THE HUMANE DIVORCE

The HUMANE DIVORCE

Breaking Up Without Breaking Down

James W. Lea, III, JD
Craig S. Galbraith, Ph.D.

WISDOM/WORK
Published by Wisdom Work
TomVMorris.com

Published 2025
Copyright © 2025

TheHumaneDivorce.com

ISBN: 979-8-9889606-8-3

Printed in the United States of America

CONTENTS

 Introduction

A Civilized and Humane Divorce

You might be considering the possibility of a divorce, or you could already have decided that this bumpy and often painful road lies ahead of you. Or you may have a close friend or family member who might need some comforting support and good advice as they move through this difficult process. If so, you're not alone. All the statistics on divorce in the U.S., if not the world, point to one conclusion—marriages fail at an alarming rate. According to recent statistics, the current percentage of first marriages that end in divorce hovers in the 40% to 45% range, with the numbers up or down a little each year for the past decade. This means that currently about 4 out of every 10 first marriages will ultimately end in divorce. And the divorce rate jumps dramatically for second and third marriages. Fifty years ago, the divorce rate was less than half of what it is now.

While divorce rates overall are different for men and women, by age group, income, and where couples live, the vast majority of people enter into a marriage with the best of intentions, with hopes of a long-lasting and rewarding relationship. Few form a marriage bond with a final objective of divorce in mind, but with the current divorce statistics the thought of it seems to bubble up occasionally, even in generally happy marriages. We all know people who have gone through a divorce. People talk about their divorces at lunch, in the gym, at work, and at family events. Usually, their stories are painful to hear. But despite its difficulties, divorce is a prominent reality in our modern world.

This book is written specifically to be a humane guide to the painful and exhausting process of divorce. We can't make a hard thing easy, but we can help you navigate the process with a more knowledgeable perspective. Nobody can change the range of emotions that arise from a marital breakup, but we believe that divorce can be approached in a civilized, thoughtful, and well informed manner. If both parties, or even one of the spouses, can view the process with a more humane sensibility, then perhaps in the end, the emotional and financial roller coaster won't be quite as bad. While there are many self-help books available on divorce, we approach the issue in a fundamentally different way. Wisdom is the key.

Using the word "humane" in our title is both intentional and critical to understanding the nature of this short book. The English term "humane" comes from the Latin *humanus* meaning "whatever is properly characteristic of human beings." In ancient times, *humanus* was associated with two important components—benevolence and knowledge, both of which are proper to humankind. The word was also used in the Old Testament Book of Wisdom in its translation from Hebrew to Latin in 382 AD. The Book of Wisdom provides a long list of the components of wisdom, and it includes the terms *humanus* (humane), *benignus* (kind), and *stabilis* (steadfast). What is wisdom then, even in the face of divorce? It means to act in a way proper to humankind, to act in a benevolent and informed manner, and to be kind and steadfast. It means being humane in all things. Wisdom is what makes civilizations civil. And this behavior refers to interactions with all parties involved in a divorce, not just a spouse or ex-spouse.

The word "humane" typically invokes important emotional behaviors such as compassion and consideration. But a deeper understanding reveals that what is at issue goes even beyond these types of positive responses. Compassion and consideration are often short-lived when a conflict becomes too difficult or it costs too much. True humaneness is a state of being, not just of feeling. It is a stable mode of presence that represents a model for what it means to be human, a standard of virtue seen in an admirable human being. It also requires, in addition to kind emotions and understanding attitudes, a deep and clear knowledge base, which is something all spouses considering divorce need to acquire. This book focuses on that knowledge and how, with its use, divorce can be a humane parting. Knowledge combined with proper behaviors is the key when it comes to the very messy and painful problem of divorce.

Second, this book is distinctive because it has two authors from very different backgrounds, and both nationally respected in their fields. Most books on divorce are written from only one perspective. And that's fine, but it's also limiting. In this book, we incorporate two of the most important components of divorce, the legal and the financial, with a concern for both understanding and managing the deep emotional issues that surround these aspects of the process. Each of us, as authors, brings our broad experience and deep knowledge to bear on these issues. And each of us has also personally experienced a divorce involving children, so we know well the emotional ups and downs of the process. It is this diversity of approaches and backgrounds, added to our relevant common experience that is unique in our book.

This book is divided into several chapters, all designed to inform the reader about the different aspects of divorce. It's a complicated and emotional journey, but it is also a legal process that must be understood and humanely managed. In chapters dealing with more legal issues, Jim Lea has taken the lead authorship role. In chapters where the topic is more financial and business in nature, Craig Galbraith has taken the lead. However, both of us have contributed to all the chapters. In our first chapter, we provide our combined observations on marriage and divorce to set the stage.

If you are thinking about ending a marital relationship, or even if you have gone so far as to talk to a divorce attorney, we recommend that you read this book as soon as you can, from beginning to end. It's a fairly easy read about an incredibly important and emotional process. If you don't have children or a business involved in the marriage, there are a few chapters you can skip. But you still might find them relevant. For any friends and family members of individuals going through a divorce, this book can also be a useful resource. It will certainly provide some insights into the difficult process that you can pass on to your friend or family member.

Finally, we need to provide the normal, required, and completely understandable, caveats. This book is meant to inform, but we do not intend to provide formal legal advice, professional psychological advice, or even official financial advice. Every state is a little different in terms of the law, and every case has its unique characteristics. Laws are constantly subject to change by rulings of higher courts, new legislation passed by state governments, and ballot initiatives. In addition, we often talk about guidelines and rules of thumb in this book and, although we try to be current in our discussions, guidelines and rules of thumb are not laws and they can differ from case to case. They can even change over time. As we mention repeatedly, because it's so important, you need to get your final legal advice from your attorney, your counseling from your therapist, and your financial information from your trusted money manager. We can certainly point you in the right direction and set the stage for asking better questions, but this book cannot be considered a replacement for personal advice from qualified professionals. It will just help to get you started in the best possible way.

Chapter 1

CAN THE MARRIAGE BE SAVED?

Thoughts from the Battlefield

It's often said that the worst things you can experience in your life are death and divorce. You don't have to be a family law attorney, marriage counselor, or therapist to hear such comments. Some people in a cynical mood add marriage to the list, which is interesting since it almost always ends in either death or divorce.

How anyone approaches and experiences these critical life events depends on how long they last, how painful they are, and perhaps most importantly, how an individual personally manages the complexities of these important life experiences. In a divorce, you can control, to a large extent, the pace, the expense, and even the pain if both parties work to exert some influence over the process in a positive way. With death, control is always ultimately taken away. In divorce, it can also be taken away from one side if the other party, or their respective lawyers, are allowed to dominate the process. Knowledge is part of what creates some measure of control. Without it, any degree of control will be lost. And if you give up all control, almost certainly you are in for a long, messy, contentious and expensive experience.

This first chapter in this book on humane divorce will focus on marriage itself, and for a good reason. There are hundreds of published studies that discuss the many causes of divorce. But from our collective experience, some shaky and difficult marriages are salvageable even at the threshold of a total breakup. It does happen, and we've seen it. But this can take place only if there is a major change, or a range of suitable adjustments, in the marriage. It's possible only when the underlying causes are honestly understood, and new goals are set.

In our combined experience in family law and divorce related finances, we have interviewed thousands of clients, each with a story about their marriage and the root causes of why it failed. We are not marriage therapists, nor are we spiritual counselors, but we do know that the first step in understanding marital failure is to understand the range of underlying problems. Once the root cause, or combination of causes, is understood, it's then possible to focus on solutions if the marriage has a chance of being saved. This is when you may need to speak to a marriage counselor or spiritual advisor.

We also know that not all root causes can be fixed. By the time a frustrated spouse speaks to a divorce attorney it's often too late—but not always. We've seen many marriages saved even at this stage, when things seemed to be beyond hope. The starting point for understanding the range of possibilities for healing the relationship must be a clear and honest reflection on the underlying problems. You can begin by asking yourself exactly why you are thinking about divorce, or are even already sitting in the reception room of a divorce attorney.

The following discussion of root causes for divorce summarizes the personal experiences of thousands of clients. Many of these causes are interrelated, and from our experience, generally the marital problems leading to a divorce are a combination of these issues. As we've mentioned, a wise and humane approach to any challenging situation must include all the relevant knowledge and understanding you can gather.

Ten Root Causes of Divorce

Root Cause #1 – Incompatibility: This is one of the most common reasons for divorce heard by lawyers when speaking with new clients. Genuine incompatibility infects, like a disease, the parties who have pledged a commitment "until death do us part." Simply put, we all want to be married to a true friend, and we need to honestly like the person we're living with. We should share common interests, attitudes, feelings, and maybe even an overlap in favorite foods.

It's often said that "opposites attract." In our professional experiences, they do sometimes, but only for a brief, passionate, and probably argumentative period—though most often, not for a lifetime. Eventually the differences arising from opposites simply wear both individuals down, along with the marriage. It's impossible to lay out the long list of things people say drive them "crazy" about their spouse. But eventually, and sometimes quickly, an actual incompatibility or uncomfortable accumulation of differences destroys the relationship.

Incompatibility can arise along many dimensions: different cultures and upbringing, conflicting emotional attitudes and personalities, different religious beliefs and spiritual orientations, disagreements about future relationship goals and family plans, and stark differences in how money is managed. Often, people come to a divorce attorney's office just plain worn down and worn out. They're tired of arguing, criticizing, or being criticized, and disagreeing over even minor differences that ultimately create frequent arguments. They're tired of sitting at the dinner table staring at the walls with nothing to say to each other. The list of reasons is almost endless, and we've heard them all.

But here is the bottom line in this: if you are just plain exhausted or worn out from the marriage experience over the long haul, you're probably done and ready for the next phase in your life. It's over and indeed it's time to move on. This can sound pessimistic, but from our experience, we're just being honest. Although you might have some love for the person on the other side of the room or now on the other side of town, but you realize you simply don't like them anymore, your marriage is probably over. Marriage counselors and psychologists might disagree, but this is our experience. Long term and deep incompatibility is a hard thing to get over, particularly since a strong marriage requires daily positive interactions and meaningful communications.

Root Cause #2 - The Inability to Respectfully Disagree: Once you stop talking, listening, or even disagreeing rationally and respectfully with your spouse, the end is likely near. Divorce attorneys hear this all the time from women clients: "He doesn't listen to me, he doesn't care, he ignores me, and he's gone all the time." From men, it's the same story but phrased differently: "She's not interested anymore in what I like and doesn't even want to hear about the things I get excited about," or "She's on me all the time, she's a nag, she's always criticizing me. I just want to get away from it." You don't have to be a divorce attorney to hear such things. Family members and friends hear them all the time. If it's caught early enough, you can bridge these differences, but a lot of people just don't, and they jump into divorce.

Take disagreeing, for example. Disagreements will always happen in a marriage. They will happen in any relationship. Research has shown there is, in fact, a right way to disagree and even to argue. The right and honest way to disagree involves a combination of behaviors. None of these are destructive, nor do they involve throwing things, smashing objects, slamming doors, hurling your own body parts into walls, or calling each other bad names. We find that name-calling is extremely destructive, more than people realize, and is often a sign of a relationship that's irreparable.

A woman understandably doesn't ever want to be called a "bitch" or a "whore" or especially not "the c-word." A man doesn't want to be called a "son-of-a-bitch," "bastard" or even described by words that might sound less extreme but hit hard at male pride, like "worthless," "lazy," "loser," or even to be described as "not making enough money." This may seem obvious, but it happens all the time in doomed marriages. Profanity, cursing, and foul language, along with intentionally hurtful words serve no positive purpose.

You can express yourself more intelligently, efficiently, and effectively, while getting across the valuable points of your position in other ways. We can often help a spouse recognize a problem, or a behavior that needs to be changed, with a tone of kindness, or at least civility, however serious the matter. But if you stop disagreeing properly, the marriage is in deep trouble. Learning how to disagree, and even argue, with more of a humane tone can often save a marriage, even when it's seriously troubled and at the point of divorce.

How to properly disagree is, in fact, a learned behavior. It's something that can be changed over time, and this is something on which marriage counselors can have a major impact. If properly addressed early enough, we find that marriages can be saved if this is the major cause of fallout. There are many excellent articles and books on how to properly disagree in a relationship. Look them up on the web. Some of our favorites are *How to Disagree* by Ian Leslie, and *Let's Just Agree to Disagree* by Craig Thomas and Jacquleine Scales. All of these can help change behaviors. Here are some of the most important ideas we have found.

- *Keep the Disagreement Focused.* Make your point and let it go quickly. Don't expand the argument to past events or broader issues. How often does an argument start over something trivial, such as what to watch on TV, then it quickly broadens to statements like "You just don't love me anymore," or even, "You never help in the kitchen," or "You ignored me last week at my parents' house, just like at that party," which could be real points of concern or contention but may have nothing to do with the original issue. Keep focused on the point at hand.

- *Let it Go.* Just let it go. It serves no purpose for a person to harbor ill feelings, apply silent treatments, or just be ill mannered for days on end. This is particularly true over what are trivial issues in the big picture of things.

- *Don't Elevate the Disagreement.* Don't let differences or arguments expand into aggressive behaviors, either verbal or physical. Escalating your arguments feeds the adrenaline cycle, and it's easy to become more emotionally aggressive as a result. Rather, be more efficient in your disagreements. And then possibly change the topic to a lighter subject and move on: "Ok. That's that. Now: What do you want to watch tonight?" or "What's your schedule tomorrow?" This is one of the most important keys—being able to let an argument end, stay on point, and to always maintain a conscious sense about when escalating attacks begin and have no productive outcome. Always stay conscious of what you say, and why you say it, and when it needs to end.

- *You Don't Always Have to Win.* We all know people who feel they simply must "win" every argument, no matter how small the issue is. These people always need to have the last word. Sometimes they seem even to enjoy an adrenaline rush from arguing, as if it's actually a fun game. They'll keep arguing *ad nauseum,* even following the other person around the house until the beleaguered spouse is simply worn down, cries, or leaves. This behavior is terribly destructive to any relationship. Prioritize the points being discussed. Is it really that important to you in the grand scheme of things? If not, then try to end on a positive note and get on to other things.

- *Turn down the Heat with the 24-hour rule.* Disagreements can become heated arguments, and these are things that can escalate. Nothing positive tends to result at this point. If you're too angry and realize that you can't properly and wisely control your own emotions in the moment, then follow this rule: Just step back. Simply drop the issue for now.

In other words, whatever the problem is, just get over it for the present and let it go, even if that takes some time. This is often a necessity in all areas of life. Don't let yourself react in kind to irritating behavior or angry comments, or to what seems like harsh criticism in real time, and don't reply in a tone you wouldn't like. Inevitably in the heat of it all, your responses will be angry and even immature. Speaking as a divorce attorney, I recommend to my clients to give anger 24 hours. I also personally try to follow this recommendation. After a suitable time, people generally have no response at all, or even a desire to respond. This works in the real world, whether in marital relationships, politics, or business. In marriage, it means coming back to your spouse later and, depending on the situation, calmly and respectfully explaining your initial words, apologizing for any excess, or even forgetting the issue completely. And I do mean 24 hours at the most. No one wants to hear in a new disagreement something they did a month ago or a year ago. That's on you for not resolving it at the time, not them.

Root Cause # 3 - Addictions: Divorce attorneys see clients every month where the root problem is alcohol and/or drug abuse. Drug abuse comes in many forms: prescribed, non-prescribed, or illicit in nature. Studies have shown that addiction accounts for about 10% of all divorces. Addiction by one spouse increases the divorce rate by a multiple of five. These are not good odds. The core problem for any addict is not the pending divorce but the addiction.

The bottom line is that most marriages generally can't survive against the evils of addictions, particularly in the long run. And we're talking about real addiction, that overriding compulsive felt need for something. And that something is always nonproductive, unhealthy, or all-consuming. Time and again, we see that addiction is stronger than the bonds of marriage. And almost by definition, addictions will become worse over time if not properly addressed.

In cases of any worsening addiction, ultimately the addicted spouse will become impossible to handle and it simply requires too much work and emotional strain for the sober spouse to even try.

All addictions have the potential to destroy a marriage if not treated and resolved in an effective manner. Frankly, a sober person can rarely live a rewarding life with an alcoholic. A normal individual simply can't endure a relationship with an untreated addict. To the addict, the next drink or fix is the most important drive in life. The marriage will not last, nor will the problem be resolved by repeated attempts at sobriety unless a permanent solution is found.

If the addiction is alcohol, we always recommend Alcohol Anonymous, or AA. Alcohol addiction is very hard to overcome, with long-term success rates low. But AA, with its peer approach to recovery, has been around for a while due to its success. Having dealt with many clients who live in an alcohol addicted marriage, AA appears to be a way of life that is often successful in saving a marriage. Other effective programs are SMART Recovery, LifeRing, Women for Sobriety, and Moderation Management. They all take slightly different approaches and work for different personalities and religious orientations. Many now have online programs. Sometimes, the cost will be covered by insurance. There are also many addiction-oriented (drug and alcohol) out-patient centers, often operated by local psychiatrists. In addition, for some addicts, live-in or residential Rehab centers can work, but these can be expensive. The key is to find a working solution in the situation, and the solution needs to be permanent.

A spouse who admits to being a drunk or an addict, then goes on short periods of help, but always "falls off the wagon," creates too many cycles of hope and disappointment for anyone to bear. Marriages will ultimately fall apart because of this behavior. From the perspective of a marriage, the addicted spouse must find a long-term solution or the other spouse will eventually give up and seek a divorce. It's well known that addicts can give up alcohol, but they will still always be alcoholics. And yet a sober alcoholic can function well in life, work, and relationships.

This also applies to both a heavily addictive use of prescribed drugs, such as barbiturates, sedatives, amphetamines, and strong opioids. And of course, serious addictions can arise from the use of the illicit drugs of fentanyl, heroin, cocaine, LSD, and meth-amphetamines like crystal meth. We have also seen marriages ending due to one spouse's heavy use of marijuana or cannabis. It's well known that the concentration of psychoactive compounds in cannabis has been steadily rising since the 1960s due to a selective breeding of potent strains, and possibly some biotechnology advances. Heavy cannabis use can be destructive to a marriage, particularly if one spouse is the sole or primary user. With drugs, if the addicted spouse doesn't keep the problem under control or abstain completely, the marriage partner will most certainly end up in a divorce attorney's office. Fortunately, like alcohol addiction, there are successful drug rehab programs and therapies that we have seen work to save marriages.

Addiction can arise in deceptive ways. It often starts with fun events, in social situations, and even as a sharing between the partners having a seemingly glorious time, but over the long run the addicted spouse dissolves into, quite frankly, a mess of a human being. We've seen where the addiction is so great that the addicted spouse is literally unable to stand or speak, even in a courtroom. At this point, the addicted person simply doesn't know or care about the other spouse, and the marriage is irrelevant. God help the marriage, but it's probably too late.

Interestingly, we've seen that occasionally when both spouses are either drinking alcoholics or drug addicts, they can somehow fade into oblivion together and maintain their marriage, although probably not very happily. We certainly don't recommend this, but we've witnessed it.

Obviously, drinking a limited amount, or even the occasional use of a recreational drug might not hurt the marriage, as long as it's not abused, becomes an addiction, or results in deep marital discord. The key is compulsion, but complete denial about its being a compulsion is a very common problem. Many clients in a divorce attorney's office will say absolutely that their spouse is addicted to alcohol or drugs, but the accused spouse insists that it's not so. In most cases, a denial of the truth of addictions will ultimately lead to divorce.

One word of caution is needed for those trying to save their marriage from the brink of divorce over this problem. If the addicted spouse has become sober, it's still a day-to-day process. Alcoholics Anonymous and other treatment programs often involve frequent meetings, close relationships with peers and sponsors, and eventually spouses. These programs are demanding. But any recovery must be, and can only be, a part of a person's life, not the dominating force. Recovery programs without question have their place in saving a marriage, but more than mere recovery will be needed for a real and healthy relationship with a spouse.

Addictions, of course, can go well beyond substance abuse. Gambling addiction is another commonly cited problem in divorce. Unlike a casual gambler who occasionally bets as a form of entertainment, a gambling disorder is a mental health condition that can be quite destructive to marriages. Betting opportunities are all around us. Lottery sales are promoted by government-sponsored TV advertisements, and tickets are available at any corner gas station. Many states and Native American reservations allow full-blown casinos. With the internet, access to online sports and casino type gambling is now readily available, even to children. Not surprisingly, gambling disorders are growing in prevalence. Current estimates put these disorders in the 5% range in the United States, with some groups, like educated young men, much higher. Chronic gambling not only impacts a family's finances, but also relationships with spouses and children. The underlying motivations behind chronic gambling are psychologically varied, such as the intense thrill of winning, trying to catch up on financial stress, a feeling of being "macho" when gaming, or simply selectively believing they can be winners in the long run, when in fact the house always wins. Like any addiction, there is assistance for these disorders.

Root Cause #4 - Infidelity: Here's a big one. Divorce attorneys can't count how many times clients have come into the office hurt and befuddled. Their spouse has just told them they no longer love them and has packed up and left. Or perhaps their spouse is in the process of leaving the marital home to "find" themselves. Confronted with such statements, clients almost always seem surprised. "Why?" they ask, and they may add, "Sure, we had our problems, but this just came out of left field." The divorce attorney will know immediately: a "third-party," and most of the time, our intuitions turn out to be right.

The causes of infidelity are many and varied and beyond this short book. However, we've seen with lots of clients that infidelity can be overcome in a marriage with an effort to find the root causes, combined with an apologetic/forgiving effort on the part of both parties. This is true even when divorce is being seriously considered. But here is the deciding point: If the cheating spouse really thinks they are "in love with the other women," or man, or if the wayward spouse sees in the new person something that shows what's been fundamentally missing from their own marriage, then the marriage is probably over.

However, this is a book on humane divorce, even in the face of infidelity. Evidence of infidelity is simply a part of the legal process. After you get whatever evidence you need, honestly confront your spouse. If they deny it but you know the truth, trouble is on the way. If they're also honest and say that they are "not in love with you anymore," then don't try to change their mind. At that point, it's probably over. This may sound harsh, but it's likely the truth, from our experiences of dealing with thousands of cases that involve a wayward partner.

However, in other cases of infidelity, there is certainly a chance of saving the marriage. Some studies show that up to 70% of married individuals cheat sometime during marriage, although other studies indicate that infidelity is lower, around 25%, but still high. The fact is that many people engage in a dalliance or two during their married lives. Is it against the vows of marriage? YES. Does it deeply hurt the other spouse? ABSOLUTELY. Does it require an effort to overcome the pain and loss of trust? CERTAINLY. But if the offending spouse truly loves the other spouse and asks for forgiveness, and if the issue can be dealt with calmly and respectfully, in the long run, the marriage can often survive.

We've seen this time and again with our clients. However, if cheating is a chronic problem, then perhaps the spouse has the type of personality that will not be changed over time, and possibly a form of "sexual addiction," "hypersexuality," or the uncontrollable need for sexual conquests. These are compulsive behaviors often involving fantasies, an obsession with pornography, and other urges that are difficult to control. There are treatments for these disorders, but they are destructive to a marriage. After all, forgiveness is wonderful on the first occasion; it's harder on the second, and much more difficult on the third, fourth, or fifteenth. And yet even then, if the offending spouse seeks professional help and seriously seeks to change, there is still hope.

Talking to thousands of spouses confronting infidelity in their marriage, if the unfaithfulness is purely physical, short-term, and really doesn't involve any deep emotion or unusually weird behaviors, the marriage can survive, with the right effort. And quite frankly, if you want to stay in your marriage, sometimes there are things better off left unsaid. Private failures need not always become a part of the public record.

Root Cause #5 - Physical and Verbal Abuse: We do not need to tell you what this is. Everybody knows it when they see it or experience it. However, people often throw around the word "abuse" far too easily, particularly when talking to a divorce attorney, as well as their friends and family. In this section, we're talking about real abuse—the ugly, mean type of repeated, escalating, and violent physical and verbal abuse of a person. Physical abuse, especially inflicted on a woman, is inexcusable. However, violence of any kind has no place in a marriage. Of course, men can also be subject to physical abuse but are often afraid to tell people. Research shows that up to 25% of women and 10% of men suffer domestic violence in their relationships. Abuse is abuse, period, and is always wrong.

In talking to clients, the combination of escalating abuse and the victim's fear of escaping is a serious problem in marriage. Remember, abused spouses can always escape, even if they emotionally think they can't. Without addressing spousal abuse in a relationship, and continuing to accept it, the problem will almost always get even worse over time, and very quickly destroy a marriage, while deeply damaging both parties as well. There are many psychological studies on spousal abuse, its causes, and possible remediation and counseling, but from our experience with abusive marriages, when it comes to physical abuse and to certain types of violent, ugly verbal abuse, people generally do not change. For whatever reason, possibly in their upbringing, their life experiences, or just their DNA, chronic violent abuse by a spousal partner seems very hard to eliminate, while keeping the marriage intact.

Often, abuse arises when the offending spouse is drunk, but when sober the very same person can be quite charming and nice. We all develop ways of coping and mixing in society. We create personality shields that we project to other people at work, at church, and to our family. These societal shields are inevitably lowered or disappear when inebriated, and the true personality comes out. There are sleepy drunks, sloppy drunks, funny drunks, talkative drunks, affectionate drunks, and even people whose personalities don't change much at all when drinking. But if violent abuse arises when a spouse has had too much to drink, you might be seeing the deep, underlying personality of that individual, a trait that's probably intrinsic to that person, regardless of what attitudes and apologies they have later when sober.

Family law attorneys find that women are particularly afraid to leave abusive relationships. In my law practice, we call it "perverse security." Change is often scary, and many people are simply frightened of risk and the unknown. It's often said that an abused spouse at least knows what to expect as they rise each day. They walk on eggshells, waiting for the next outburst, criticism, and verbal or physical assault. Or in private, they have a real fear of the next time the spouse has too much to drink. A true marriage doesn't survive long in these circumstances. Violent words can hurt almost as much as fists, and fists often follow an escalation of violent verbal abuse. To stay in that is not security, but itself a sickness. But this can be cured.

When it comes to true, chronic physical abuse, our advice about a potential divorce is: Leave! Damn the consequences, and the gray cloud will ultimately be lifted. Look at yourself hard in the mirror each morning. Are you happy? Do you love the person in the next room? Are you really the problem that your abusive spouse says you are? Be honest with yourself. You are not the problem when abuse is involved. Unlike addiction caught early, and even infidelity caught eventually, real abuse is extremely hard, if not impossible, to overcome in a marriage.

Root Cause #6 - Psychological Disorders: The American Psychological Association has published for years a detailed description of psychological disorders in their *Diagnostic and Statistical Manual of Mental Disorders*. Not surprisingly, it's a long list. If you were to read these descriptions, you might spot your spouse somewhere in the details or even realize you're seeing yourself in a mirror. Many of these disorders are common throughout the world's population.

They can be addressed and treated. Minor disorders, if treatable, should elicit nothing but compassion, support, and understanding from a spouse, if there is still love in the marriage.

For example, anxiety disorders are very common in today's high-pressure world. The Anxiety and Depression Association of America reports that about 15 million adults in the U.S. experience anxiety disorders, with 6 million having actual panic attacks. If you or your spouse think an anxiety disorder is at play in your marriage, read the detailed description of the condition in the APAs *Diagnostic and Statistical Manual of Mental Disorders*. And talk to a qualified professional. Since so many people experience symptoms of anxiety disorders and these can be effectively treated, they are really no reason to blow up a marriage. The same can be said for a variety of other treatable disorders, such as depression, obsessive compulsion disorder, and even borderline personality disorders.

However, from our experience of dealing with family law, there are some disorders a marriage probably can't survive and maybe shouldn't. We certainly don't claim to be experts in diagnosing these disorders, but their impact on marriages is seen every week in the offices of divorce attorneys. Severe mental disorders such as schizophrenia or psychopathy are obvious. Anything that leads to sexual child abuse or other genuinely perverse behaviors would count. There are some people who are just beyond help from a relationship point of view. From the perspective of marriage and divorce, a malignantly narcissistic personality disorder hovers close to the edge, since to an extreme narcissist, they are all that matter in a relationship. Such individuals are obsessed with their success or their looks, they need mirrors and flatterers everywhere, they need to feel important, and they're prone to criticize others constantly. They can never see or admit it when they've made a mistake. And all of that is tough on a marriage.

Schizophrenics simply do not have much touch with reality and are destructive to any type of relationship. Sociopaths are utterly unfeeling, uncaring, and do not feel any guilt over what they do to others. These types of people can also be very cunning, even charming, and can easily fool the people around them. You can be married to a sociopath for years and not really know it until you find your self-esteem and self-worth beaten to a bloody pulp. We won't describe these types of people in any more detail because entire books have been written on their personalities.

But be careful about casually using these categories. Clients on the verge of divorce often label their spouses with these severe disorder titles. Remember, however, that personality disorders are real mental health conditions, and ultimately need to be diagnosed by trained professionals to be properly identified and treated. Reading something on the web or even in this book that sounds like your spouse might get you wondering, but this is not a definitive diagnosis. You will also want to talk to a licensed psychotherapist. But if it's true that your spouse has such a problem, then do some serious thinking about the future of the marriage.

Root Cause #7 - Sex and Affection: Sex can enhance or destroy a marriage, and yet in the end may not matter at all. So much is made of it. It depends on who you are and what you need. The fact of life is that as people get older, male and female, nature has a way of impacting sexual performance, desire, and ability. This is not a reflection of love or affection, but simply the unfortunate (or to some, fortunate) results of aging. Illness, injury, and chronic pain can also impact this issue. One of the authors of this book does extensive economic loss analysis in cases of personal injury and has interviewed hundreds of injured and disabled individuals over the past forty years. Without question, injury and chronic pain can immensely affect the ability to have or enjoy sex. Even the slightest chronic pain in the back and knees can mess things up in the bedroom. Migraine headaches or severe head injuries are also devastating.

Research has shown that many psychological issues, and even PTSD, can make having sex difficult or even distressing, given felt pressures to perform. This should not be an indication of loss of affection or reduced love. In addition, it can be extremely frustrating to the injured individual who still might have the passion, but not the means. There are always other alternatives to classic intercourse in the bedroom. This needs to be understood and managed by both partners, and it inevitably involves honest communication about issues we tend to keep personal and very private. But the one thing a marriage cannot survive is lack of affection and communication. A kiss on the cheek, a warm hug, or holding hands on the way to a movie can mean a lot. Don't let basic affection die. Don't let it fade away.

Root Cause #8 - Financial Problems: Home finances are pretty simple in theory: The household needs to make more money than it spends, or at least that needs to equal out. Spending less money than you make allows for savings, some insurance for future unforeseen events, and an eventual retirement. But research indicates that financial problems are one of the top five reasons for divorce. So, what's the problem? We see several different types of financial issues with our clients.

First, generally under most state laws, earned income from the spouses, regardless of who earns it, is generally considered marital. That's also the way people in a strong marriage tend to look at it. This is the proper, humane and civilized perspective on marital finances. It doesn't mean you can't have separate accounts, if that works. It doesn't mean that one person can't do all the bookkeeping and pay the bills. Likewise, it doesn't imply that every purchase online or in a store must have the explicit approval of the other spouse. The key is that, emotionally, it all needs to be considered and understood as part of the marital whole—and particularly, in the case of major items. This means emotionally understanding that regardless of who makes the most money, all the household income is marital. This eliminates many of the financial problems that can occur in a marriage.

The second problem is that the family unit simply spends too much money to make ends meet. We see this whether people are rich, middle class, or poor. It's almost like a competition over who can spend the most. Some family units habitually spend too much money, and over time this often leads to divorce. We are often stunned by the spending behaviors of some of our clients. In one recent divorce case, a local physician brought over one million dollars a year into the household, yet amazingly the family unit consistently spent even more money annually on a fancy house by the beach, expensive sports cars, and a sequence of almost continuous vacationing at pricey resorts and summer homes. They ate out every night at fancy restaurants, remodeled their home frequently, had private schools and sports lessons for the kids, cosmetic surgeries for both spouses, and numerous club memberships, to the point that they ultimately had no money left at the end of each month. Marriages in trouble, regardless of income levels, often exhibit this compulsion to spend, spend, and spend more, to the point of financial ruin. And this ultimately places great stress on the marriage.

The third money problem we see is related, but here it's clearly pointed more at one guilty party. In this case, one spouse simply spends household money frivolously and carelessly and often without the other even knowing about it. Men spend on getting the new golf clubs, more video games, jet skis, fancy clothes, expensive watches, fun cars, or on pricey hobbies. Or it can be spent on more questionable items such as gambling losses or buying too many lottery tickets. For women, it can be a shopping compulsion or over-spending on personal care products and activities. Online ordering has made this incredibly easy. Credit card debt increases, bills don't get paid, and suddenly the other spouse finds out. There's nothing wrong with having fun and spending money impulsively at times, but it needs to be controlled, not one-sided, not secretive, and within the limits of the family budget.

The final financial problem we often see is when one spouse, typically but not always the one earning the most money, excessively and maliciously budgets the other spouse into unhappiness. This happens a lot. We constantly hear complaints that the targeted spouse is only given a small budget or allowance, while the higher earning spouse controls all the money. This almost always is indicative of other issues, such as an excessively controlling personality, and not fundamentally understanding the marital nature of income in a marriage. Controlling money is, indeed, felt as a source of power. And it creates problems.

What's interesting is that compared to the other issues in this chapter, financial differences are probably the easiest to fix. Simply learn to view all income earned as marital. Get the help of a financial planner if you need to. But above all, discuss income and expenses, budget cooperatively, don't hide money, be honest about purchases, and be respectful of the other person's spending opinions and priorities, even if that spouse isn't the primary income producer.

And always remember that a non-income earning spouse is probably doing the housework, working in the garden, beautifying the environment, raising the kids, keep up social friendships, washing laundry, cooking, and generally seeking to keep things orderly and nice. These activities all contribute financially to the marriage in a real way. To an economist, this is called "household service production," and economists can put a very real value on this type of work.

Root Causes #9 and #10: Loss of Trust and Respect: These issues go hand and hand. If you don't trust your spouse, you have likely lost all respect for them. The loss of these two attitudes which lie at the core of a marriage results from, in large part, three things: Infidelity, money, and abuse. Loss of trust can also occur if one spouse falsely and chronically accuses the other spouse of things that are not true, even if ridiculous on the surface, such as stealing cash, car keys, mail or jewelry, when all the accusing spouse did was misplace something and then forgot. False accusations of infidelity destroy trust and respect almost as much as cheating itself. Constant jealousy inevitably manifests a lack of trust and respect between partners. Marriage involves a whole list of responsibilities, many of which are listed in the marriage vows. Within all this, trust and respect are built over time. If one or both spouses fail in their responsibilities to the marriage, either through bad decisions or habitually unhealthy behaviors, trust and respect will start to evaporate, and so will the bonds that hold together your marriage.

Thoughts on Marriage and Divorce

It is not our job to pontificate to the world. We're simply focused on providing useful insight into healthy marriage and humane divorce. And we hope that if you find our words helpful, you'll share our kind intent in offering to others what you learn here. If someone asks for help, then by all means freely give it. You may decide your spouse has a problem, but they often won't agree. Remember, people always justify their behaviors to themselves at the time they are making poor and even unethical decisions. They also continue to justify it most of the time afterward. So, pointing a finger rarely works. If the issues discussed in this chapter can't be engaged fruitfully and bridged, your marriage will likely dissolve. Abandoning things, places, and people that you once enjoyed and loved in order to escape a destructive relationship may keep you emotionally sober, but in the process, you will likely lose some of the friends, moments, and activities that kept you intact as a person in the first place. In the end, however, if relinquishing those things keeps you emotionally healthy, then choose emotional health over marriage. And this choice, which is necessary at times, will most likely and ultimately involve divorce. After all, you have to live and you deserve to be happy, whether your spouse ever comes to agree on what that requires or not.

In our many years of experience, marriages can overcome most of the above reasons for divorce, with the exception of perhaps violent abuse, chronic addictions and a true lack of love, but it will take work, possibly professional therapy, and real change. And it will require both spouses to be committed. One spouse alone can't save a marriage.

If a spouse who has had an affair still loves you, you can forgive them and move along. If a spouse has a substance use problem with either drugs or alcohol, and if they can become sober and live a clean life, they can be a good partner. Money issues can be managed if both parties understand the commitment to marital financial equity. If a spouse has a treatable disorder, such as anxiety, depression or any other of the common disorders, a marriage can survive it.

Professional help is available in all these areas, whether in the form of marriage counselors, spiritual and religious advisors, financial planners, alcohol and drug rehab programs, psychologists and therapists. They can all be effective if both parties make a serious effort, even when the marriage is at the point of talking to divorce attorneys. But these efforts require understanding, care, and compassion by both parties. Unfortunately, if one or both spouses are not inclined to work seriously on these issues, then the inevitability of divorce is on the horizon.

Inexplicably, other than true domestic abuse and the worst psychological disorders, what a marriage cannot survive is what many might perceive to be the simplest of problems, a deep incompatibility and loss of love. On some level you will need to have as much in common with your spouse as you can and many shared interests. Some people just marry the wrong person for them. The reason they split up is that simple. They were never supposed to get married in the first place.

Unfortunately, most couples on the verge of divorce will put it off for reasons they may feel rise above their own happiness. Sometimes it's religion or family pressures, often it's for the children, and sometimes it's a real concern for their financial future. Quite often, it's simply a fear of change. People tend to acclimate to an environment even when there are fundamental issues at play because the prospect of facing the world on your own is frightening.

The purpose of this book is to simply give you a guide as you move through the possibility or actual reality of a divorce, hopefully in the most humane manner possible. We have underlined the many opportunities for salvaging a marriage on the verge of divorce. But there is a warning here also. Don't continue to reside in the empty shell of a fundamentally ruined marriage that will not only ultimately destroy you, your faith, and your perspective on life's worth, but also your relationships with the important people in your life who care about you.

Chapter 2

HOW TO CHOOSE A GOOD DIVORCE LAWYER

It Takes a Bit of Effort

I like to solve problems or at least attempt that. This is why I ultimately fell into being a divorce lawyer. But I've always questioned why I got into it in the first place or continued to practice, even after more than forty years in the field. I played varsity sports in high school in North Carolina and have tried to stay competitively and physically active since. My co-author, Craig, has the same attitude. He played high school sports in San Diego growing up, receiving several athletic scholarship offers to attend college, but he joined the army instead. Later in college after his service, he played on the varsity tennis and fencing teams.

I personally think an athletic background and drive is part of it. Sports bring out my competitiveness, which for me means long hours of preparation, study, and work and finally the big game, the performance. This attitude of preparation for the big game translates well to the courtroom. Most of the few clients who have given up on me simply had unreasonable expectations, no matter what was said to them. When people expect too much, regardless of what their attorney tells them, the attorney almost always becomes the target of their outrage. On occasion, I deserve and acknowledge it. Any divorce attorney, if honest, will admit this.

Kris Kristofferson once wrote, "I'm a walking contradiction, partly truth, partly fiction." In short, that's a domestic lawyer. As one famous family lawyer said, with more than a grain of exaggeration, "We are doing a thankless job for the ungrateful masses." This will likely elicit a smile or chuckle from other lawyers, but it's not actually always true. It's just a great quote capturing what one side of the divide sometimes thinks. There's really a great deal of satisfaction in this job, particularly when working with grateful and kind clients while they are going through extremely difficult situations. There are also big disappointments, anxieties, and pressures associated with the job. If I had to put a percentage on it, 80% to 90% of clients are great people, with the remaining 10% to 20% being folks who'd drive any normal human being insane. Perhaps that's a part of the reason they're getting a divorce.

Lawyers who typically deal with divorce related issues are called divorce attorneys, domestic law attorneys, or family law attorneys. Many of them appear on the "best attorneys lists." There are other attorneys who do not appear on the various prestige lists but are still great at what they do. The following are the qualities of a good domestic lawyer. These are the characteristics that you need to look for and find if you're seeking representation.

The Peculiar Personalities of Domestic Attorneys

Personal Characteristic - Smart and Quick. Domestic attorneys need to be smart. That's probably obvious, since to become an attorney at all, you need to have a pretty good mind. So, intelligence itself isn't really the issue. After all, attorneys typically graduate from college, then spend three years in graduate law school to get their JD, then pass the state bar exam. But being smart or intelligent doesn't make a person "quick." Not all lawyers are quick in applying their intelligence. Medieval philosophers long ago saw this important difference. Quickness is the ability to rapidly and creatively apply intelligence when confronted by uncertain and new situations. Quickness is the basis of intuition, or maybe it's the other way around. Domestic law, by its very nature, is complex, fast-moving and highly charged. Often, major issues pop up at the last minute, evidence will change overnight, and clients can become incredibly emotional and unpredictable. A good domestic attorney will then need to pivot in an instant and know which direction to head. This takes a combination of intelligence and quickness. Keep this in mind when meeting an attorney for the first time. Get a sense of how quick they are on their feet, intellectually, how rapidly they process information and respond well to what you're saying, and not just with old, general, well-worn phrases they could repeat in their sleep.

Personal Characteristics - Slightly Crazy. Few lawyers actually like trial work, regardless of what they say. It's a situation of great pressure. And even fewer think about wandering into the dreaded field of domestic law. Just as a "domestic disturbance" can be one of the most difficult situations for police officers to enter, a domestic divorce is not the easiest thing to handle. By its very nature, domestic law tends to attract attorneys who are perhaps a little peculiar at times, a little "out there," and on the edge. But you may need a bit of a character to see you through all the ups and downs and ins and outs of the process with a measure of success.

Personal Characteristic – Fair, Professional, and Situation Oriented. A good domestic attorney is always trying to do their best professionally, respectfully, and efficiently. Their main obligation is not to just get the job done, but to get it done in the best way possible. A good domestic attorney is honest and will tell you the truth from the beginning, not just what you want to hear. Such an attorney is not afraid for you to walk out after the first hour. Good attorneys have plenty of good clients. You won't offend the lawyer by going elsewhere. And, of course, you need to feel comfortable about the fit. But if you do walk out because you don't like what the attorney has told you, make sure you're being reasonable. If you shop around long enough, you might eventually find a lawyer who will cater to your every whim and hope until you, in an eventual state of shock, don't get anything near the results you expected. If recommended attorneys keep telling you that your expectations are probably too high, then it might be good to do some self-reflection and consider the possibility that they might be right.

Personal Characteristic – Prepared and Well Versed in Many Aspects of the Law. Good domestic attorneys are not only thoroughly prepared, but they need to have a broad understanding of all the relevant laws and other issues. By their very nature, domestic cases involve a variety of legal, personal, and economic matters—families have children, they own real estate, they operate small businesses, they have earned pensions, they have different types of investments, and have bought furniture, and cars, and boats. Families going through divorce have emotional problems, financial considerations, and may have other legal issues, such as any criminal or civil matters that might impact the case. Marriages in trouble often involve someone hiding assets, a lying partner, and just common trickery. A good domestic attorney needs to know enough about these different aspects of life to deal with other attorneys. They also need enough knowledge to work with clients from all walks of life, ask pertinent questions, and cross-examine a range of real estate, financial, and accounting experts who might testify. When a domestic lawyer gets to the courtroom, they must be prepared, intimately know the law, and have great quick instincts about everything that's going on in the courtroom.

Personal Characteristic – Relationship with the Court System. Attorneys in any field can get a bad reputation within the court system. However, a good attorney needs to work in the system to get the best results. Good attorneys are friendly to the clerks and the bailiff, and respectful to the judge. A good domestic attorney will get in and out of the case quickly and as efficiently as possible. I'm always amazed at clients who stand by just watching as their lawyer is literally infuriating everyone in a courtroom. Some attorneys ask repeated, monotonous, and mundane questions. They repeat a direct examination on cross examination, they make ineffective and ill-prepared arguments, and the client who is not around courtrooms a lot is often thinking that person is doing a good job. Relentlessly banging away during a repetitious cross examination is the epitome of poor lawyering. I wish prospective clients could take prospective attorneys out for a "test drive" and witness their normal courtroom behavior to get a sense of their degree of professionalism or utter lack in that area. But recommendations from sensible former client help.

Domestic attorneys, except perhaps in the largest cities, generally cater to a small cadre of family court judges who work in the region and who all previously practiced law. Even in large cities like New York that have family court systems, the number of family judges is still relatively small. These judges know the law and they know a good lawyer when they see one. As attorneys, we are not there to entertain the client or anyone else. Most good lawyers won't make every pointless argument just to be called a "bulldog," or seek to impress a client into thinking how tough they are, when it might be counterproductive. A good domestic attorney won't antagonize a judge with lots of mundane points, leaving him or her bored and irritated. Good attorneys can certainly have different approaches in court, but at some point, there's a line to be drawn when conduct starts to hurt the case. A trial isn't about the attorney, but the result.

Finding the Gem of an Attorney – The Fit

Any lawyer in turn will have both good clients and bad clients. It's in every client's own interest to seek to be a good one. Most clients in domestic cases will have very high expectations, if not demands. We have heard these hundreds of times—they want to have complete custody of the children, they don't want to give up any of the pension they earned over twenty years of marriage, they even want to "screw" their ex-spouse in retaliation for something, they want to immediately see or speak with their attorney at all hours and all times. The list is endless. When it doesn't turn out that way, those clients get mad. They post negative comments on social media. They even sue their attorneys and report them to the State Bar Association. That just comes with the profession. So don't believe everything you read or hear, as you seek to find the right lawyer to represent you.

Personally, I don't fraternize with many other lawyers after hours; not because I don't like them or I think they're bad people, but because I see them all week at work. Lots of them join social clubs, play golf together, and regularly socialize with other attorneys and their families. But what matters most is how they treat each other and their clients in their work. To find a good lawyer, you don't have to find one who is close friends with all the other lawyers in town. You do need one known to treat others with respect and in a humane way.

How then do you find a good lawyer? There are some bona fide and legitimate sources for your search to find a good respectable attorney to represent you. Our recommendation is to use a combination of sources that are helpful.

1. Look Up Attorney Ratings in Publications. Just like almost any professional field, there are several publications that list, if not rank, attorneys.

Martindale Hubbell Law Directory-Avvo (Including Lawyers. com, Nolo, Ngage Live Chat, and Captorra): These two listing agencies have teamed up. One is old and respected, the other newer and gaining respect. *Martindale Hubbell* is the oldest and most respected lawyer rating service ever put together. Many clients have no idea of its existence. *Martindale Hubbell* was founded in 1868 to provide information to the legal industry. They have been publishing the *Martindale-Hubbell Law Directory* since 1931 in book form, and more recently on the web. Its ratings come from other lawyers and judges, the toughest scrutiny any lawyer can experience. These ratings are pretty accurate and reliable. Note, however, that some lawyers refuse to be rated. This is their choice, so although the *Martindale Hubbell Law Directory* can be considered a good source, it's not a fully comprehensive one. If someone is not rated in the *Martindale Hubbell Law Directory*, they still might be a good and suitable attorney.

The *Directory* has the following ratings:

- **A Rating:** The lawyer is preeminent in his or her field and considered the best of the best. If you see a lawyer rated A with fifteen to twenty years of experience, you're probably in good hands. With twenty to forty years of experience, an A-rated lawyer is still at the top in his or her field. These lawyers make up approximately 5% of the entire Bar.
- **B Rating:** Good lawyers may never achieve an A rating. B rated attorneys work hard and do a good job. If they have achieved a B rating between ten and twenty years of practice, they have a good chance of going on to an A rating. These people are still good lawyers even in their twenty, twenty-fifth, thirty and thirty-fifth years. They have worked hard and will represent you well.
- **C Rating:** There are young, dynamic and good lawyers in this category. It takes about five years to even warrant a rating, so nothing is wrong with this rating if your attorney is relatively young. If you see a lawyer in *Martindale Hubbell* who has been practicing less than ten years but has gained a C rating, you can count on the fact that this lawyer is on his or her way up. If you want to save some money and

have a young dynamic attorney, these lawyers may be it for you. If the lawyer has been practicing for more than twenty years and still receives a C rating, then frankly it sometimes raises questions. If lawyers in *Martindale Hubbell* have been practicing less than twelve years, they have taken a chance at a rating. As a client, you can probably take a chance with them.

- **V Rating:** A "V" next to a rating means a "very high ethical" rating, in addition to the rating for ability. Take that for what it's worth.

One last cautionary point should be made about *Martin Hubbell Law Directory's* ratings, or any ratings-based publication. There are some lawyers who know how to play the rating game. They might be masquerading with an A rating attached to the firm, even though the A rating belongs to another long and established lawyer in the firm. Some lawyers with no rating employ this as a marketing strategy, to continue to use the name of a formerly A-rated but now retired attorney. Playing the ratings game is misleading and unfair to the client. If you find an A rated firm, or an A rated lawyer, be sure to check whether they are still practicing and specifically check the status of the attorneys who are working under this A rating.

Best Lawyers in America and U.S. News: U.S. News and World Report, as they do in areas of medicine and education, provides a service known as *Best Lawyers in America*. If a domestic attorney makes it to this publication, they are very likely one of the best in the field. *U.S. News and World Report* has now included the best law firms in America. There are a lot, some 5,000 in number, so you can probably find one in your area. This is a relatively new service following along the lines of the *Report's* publications in other areas. It's strictly on the web. If a lawyer is listed in this service, they are probably pretty good at what they do. But remember, there are good attorneys who are not listed. A word of caution is that this service also lists the overall number of attorneys in a firm. If it pops up that a firm has 300 attorneys, this is most probably for the whole national practice, not just in the local office in your area.

Super Lawyers: Terrible name, good service. I know the names picked year to year, and these lawyers are generally good. This guide seems pretty reliable, but use it only in combination with other services.

Other Lawyer Listing Services: Regarding all the rest, in my opinion, be cautious for now. These lawyer services have a long way to go to reach high levels of credibility within the field. Some are legitimate and are trying to improve, but many other listing services are just paid advertising.

2. Word of Mouth. Everybody knows somebody who has gone through the adventure of a divorce. Ex-clients of attorneys love to talk. In the domestic field, you always hear mixed reviews about lawyers. A friend once asked me how it feels to have half the town hate me. This is a fact in the experience of a domestic attorney in any community. The other side won't like you because you got way too much. Your own clients won't think you got enough. Client expectations often far exceed what the law allows. And people end up paying a lot to find this out. When talking to people about recommendations, don't ask just one person, ask ten. If a name is repeated as being a good lawyer perhaps five times out of the ten, you're probably in good hands. And always take any advice you can get from the clerks, bailiffs, and any judges you may know, because they have been in the courtroom and are highly reliable sources. Word of mouth should not be used alone, but in combination with other recommendations.

3. Talk to Experts. A really good source of information is to talk with the experts, if you can find one who works with local attorneys

on divorce cases. These include forensic economists, business valuators, accountants, investment advisors, real estate appraisers, and
therapists. Most of these experts have worked with several different attorneys in the region. Such experts are generally well educated and professional in nature. Since they are professionals, don't
expect them to discredit anyone overtly, but they might give a positive recommendation or two, depending on your specific issues
and situation. Pay attention to what they say.

Attorneys, just like in any profession, have strengths and weaknesses. Some are great in court, and others might work better with
child issues, while yet other attorneys may better understand issues
involving businesses and complex finances. Some attorneys appear
to work better with either the female or male perspective, and some
are meticulously slow, while other attorney offices just seem to move
more quickly. Also, some lawyers charge more than others. Often,
it's the outside experts who assist in divorce situations who know the
true personalities, strengths, and weaknesses of the different attorneys in your town, depending on the nature of the case. You do yourself a favor by finding them and asking them for recommendations.

4. Advertising. Advertising has always been controversial in the
legal profession. You tend to see it a lot more in personal injury
law than domestic law. In my opinion, advertising means very little in the domestic field unless a lawyer can advertise with factual
credentials, like a rating from the *Martindale Hubbell Law Directory*. Often you'll see an advertisement claiming that a particular law office will "Fight for You," or some similar statement pro-
jecting toughness. All lawyers will "fight for you," which is their
job regardless of what the advertising says. "Fighting for you" is a
meaningless phrase for any type of attorney, just like an OBGYN
advertising "We Deliver!" which of course should not be taken to
imply that other OBGYNs don't deliver babies.

What's important for divorce attorneys is that they should be
masters of the rules, regulations, laws, and procedures in detail.

They need to know how to effectively work within the system. A good attorney also truly understands the personal needs of the client. They have the ability to negotiate a possible settlement and, perhaps above all, a good attorney gives wise advice. But if the case is absolutely going to court, then you need to find a good and experienced trial attorney. These important characteristics of a good domestic attorney are almost impossible to communicate in advertising, whether on TV, billboards, or the web. In fact, we find that many lawyers' websites contain misleading information in a promotional way. First and foremost, look and see if the actual lawyer is the one speaking to you in a video pitch, and not a hired actor. That will give you the opportunity to size up the lawyer you are considering. Read carefully the information you're receiving and be sure you're getting accurate information.

5. Second Language Issues. One of our wives is a native Spanish-speaking professional, born and raised in Puebla, Mexico. She has studied in England, Spain, and Switzerland, and is fluent in several languages. She's now a faculty member in the Spanish department at a highly rated regional university, and regularly translates legal documents written in Spanish, as well as acting as a court interpreter for Spanish in domestic cases. If a case involves Spanish, or any other language, and one of the party's English is spotty, and especially if this is you, then these are our recommendations.

1. Bring your own skilled Spanish-speaking or other relevant language translator with you to the attorney's office, for at least the first meeting. This can be a friend you trust or a family member. That way you can better converse with the attorney and paralegals, and if the attorney's office has a translator, you can determine how good they are.
2. If you don't know anybody to help, be sure to ask if the attorney has a Spanish speaking person on staff or has good access to a Spanish translator for the meetings and possi-

bly the trial. There are now online interpretation systems that any attorney can access. In larger cities you can almost always find an attorney who is bilingual. In small communities it may be harder.

3. Understand that there will be a lot of legal and perhaps financial terms discussed. It's critically important that the translator you use is qualified in legal and financial translation. We have found that many translators don't really have a good grasp of sophisticated terms and concepts. They might know basic language translation and street lingo, but not high-level and complicated legal terminologies and translations. This is important. There are many translators and interpreters, but few can honestly work with the sophisticated terminology of law, business, and economics.

This last point is critical. For example, one time, just sitting in court waiting for a case to be called up, we were listening to the trial going on before us. The court-appointed interpreter was so bad, we couldn't take it anymore. What the person was testifying on the stand was simply not being communicated to the judge. We stood up in the courtroom, politely interrupted the proceedings, and told the judge about the translation issues. The judge asked some quick questions and then fired the court-appointed translator on the spot. We have both seen this happen more than once, not only in criminal cases but also domestic cases. Remember, everybody, including judges and attorneys, wants to make sure that all parties understand what is being said in both general discussions and in the court room.

6. The Personal Visit. Like in any business, presentation means a lot. Domestic lawyers are usually small firm practitioners or have a relatively small office within a larger firm. You need to be properly impressed with what you see—the decor, paintings, and furniture should add-up to a polished and professional environment. This will let you know whether the lawyer has been successful. You will find an appealing ambiance in any large law firm you walk into that has a domestic section, but be prepared to pay, because there's a lot of overhead for such a firm.

A one-on-one interview with your lawyer is important. Glance around the attorney's office. Their desk should be a little crowded and maybe even a bit messy. This is a hallmark of a busy lawyer. The rest of the office should be clean, presentable, and nicely decorative. The office needs to impress you, or at least not raise red flags. It's not impressive to look around and see boxes and notes piled randomly throughout the office. Is the place clean or are there old food stains and gum wrappers on the floor? This lets you know that things are not getting done.

Take a good hard look also at the lawyer you're considering. Is he or she well-dressed? This is our uniform. We're always on call and it's necessary that we can spring into action at a moment's notice. All attorneys don't need to wear a suit and tie to the office, but they should generally be professionally attired, and appropriately for their client base.

Be sure that you at least click in some personal way with your lawyer. For example, one of the co-authors knows a domestic attorney in Ocean Beach, California, an edgy coastal community in San Diego, who focuses on the beach and surfing community. He's a surfer himself and closes his office at 4pm when "the surf is up." In the office, he dresses casually like a surfer, and his wall is covered with beach art. He even keeps his surfboards in his office. He's a good attorney, but his office and personal attire are clearly targeted toward his primary client base. That's the key. But he does wear a suit and tie to court. Cowabanga!

You don't have to be your lawyer's best friend, nor does your lawyer need to be the greatest and most remarkable person you've ever met. But they need to appear highly competent and capable of doing the job you want them to do at a personal level. You need to feel comfortable with them under circumstances that are naturally filled with stress, tears, and even heartbreak. It's always nice to have a doctor with a charming bedside manner, but the key issues are whether they listen to you, and whether they can get the job done. The same is true for any professional, whether it's your accountant, mechanic, plumber, dentist, or gardener. You need someone who does quality work.

What to Initially Expect From your Lawyer

When you engage an attorney, it's very reasonable to have certain expectations. Not every expectation can be met, but there are some expectations that are sensible. Every domestic attorney should provide the following when you initially engage them.

1. In your initial conference with a domestic lawyer you should expect the truth, whether you like it or not. A lawyer simply telling you what you want to hear is just trying to get your business. As an example, I have often had clients walk in and say they want to protect their pension after a long marriage. In most cases, that is not possible. Pensions earned during the marriage are most likely to be considered a marital asset and divided with your spouse. Clients will also walk in and say they do not want to pay alimony. In most cases, that may not be possible if they have provided for their spouse throughout the course of their marriage. It is perfectly OK to raise these issues but hear the answer.

2. Expect a thorough explanation of the law and a candid assessment of your case. It's your right as a client to have at least a fundamental understanding of the process you are about to go through.

3. Again, look around your lawyer's office, including its organization and appearance. Believe it or not, this does matter. You

want to go to court with a lawyer who looks put together
and ready to mediate or try your case.

4. Assess how comfortable you are with the lawyer's staff.
    The staff are the people you will have contact with most
    often throughout your case. The attorney will need to have a
    friendly and engaging staff you can embrace in times of crisis.
    A lawyer can't be available twenty-four hours a day. They are
    often on the phone, meeting other clients, working on case
    documents, present in court or mediation, or just generally
    solving people's problems. Anyone who is rude and conde-
    scending to the staff will only hurt their own case. Remember,
    many times you'll interact with the staff, such as reception-
    ists and paralegals, more than even the attorney, periodical-
    ly during your case. This is particularly true when collecting
    and organizing the necessary documents. And it's generally
    the staff who will pass your communications to the attorney.
    Receptionists and paralegals are the conduit to access. They
    are on your side and merit your respect and kindness.

5. Thoroughly discuss fees and what the expectation of fees will
    be in the future.

6. Generally, expect a return phone call on the day you make a
    call. There are exceptions to this, for example if the attorney
    is in the middle of a complex case. In this situation, a paralegal
    might call back. Ask your lawyer specifically about their phone
    call policy, both in terms of timing and expenses. Talking on
    the phone, even with paralegals, is generally billable time. In
    domestic cases, you should watch carefully how much time
    your lawyer is spending on your needs. A good attorney
    should be able to put together the documents necessary for
    court in quick fashion, depending on the complexity of the
    case. They will also know not to waste the court's time and
    try only an efficient case.

7. Talk openly about the opportunity for settlement or media-
    tion. Settling cases in an informal manner is usually the best

option and is certainly the least expensive. Mediation is also an important part of trying to resolve a divorce, particularly in a humane manner. In many states, an effort at mediation is required before a case goes to court. Everybody should be prepared at the time of mediation and not then ask for documents from the other side. Asking for documents at the last minute probably means they've not conducted a full and proper discovery. In these cases, some attorneys are just using the mediation as a discovery process. It's a waste of everybody's time. The mediation should have only the purpose of resolving your case, not simply prolonging it. Talk about these different paths on the first day.

8. Monitor carefully the time it takes your lawyer to get through the case. Many delays are dictated by the court calendar and are beyond your attorney's control. Delays can also be caused by the stubbornness of your spouse and their lawyers. But be sensitive enough to recognize it if your lawyer is also wasting time and just aggravating the situation.

9. I have a Golden Rule in domestic cases. Not everybody follows this, but I find it very important. I will not send an e-mail or letter to another lawyer that cannot be forwarded to the client on the other side, verbatim. I often get inflammatory e-mails. Forwarding such communication to my client usually just aggravates the situation. You and your lawyer are free to sit together in private and talk as disparagingly about the other side as you want. However, if you convey those negative remarks in e-mails to the other side, you'll simply inflame the situation. And that's rarely helpful. Such derogatory e-mails and other communications might also be held against you in a child custody hearing. No matter how obstinate or difficult your ex-spouse may be, it does you no good to engage him or her in negative ways unless advised to do so by your lawyer. Follow the lead of the professionalism it takes to get through the process amicably, if you possibly can.

10. The Bulldog. Lots of lawyers get the reputation of being a "bulldog." These practitioners are often not liked by other lawyers and judges. We've mentioned this already, since it's important. There's no problem with being assertive, but an attorney needs to do so in a professional way. If it's obvious that your lawyer is irritating the hell out of both the lawyer on the other side and the judge, you've probably made a bad choice. And it's still within your right to express your concern if you see this happen. A good lawyer should listen to what you say. But also remember that a professional attorney will honestly tell you when you're wrong. Don't expect your own lawyer to agree with everything you say, or to do whatever you tell them to do. That's not their role. Remember, they're the experts. But do speak up if it seems that their conduct does is not conducive to a good result.

Take note of your comfort level with the attorney you are sitting with in their office. Even with the best lawyers, there can be personality conflicts. It might be nobody's fault—it just doesn't click. It doesn't feel right. If you begin to feel uncomfortable with your lawyer, do feel free to seek another one. However, if you continuously jump from lawyer to lawyer, it reflects on you, not the lawyers. If you had a "good lawyer," as established by the community in the first place, it can certainly reflect on you if you leave. If you have disagreements, discuss them honestly with your attorney. If your attorney is in any way perpetuating these problems, unless his or her position is warranted, it's time to get a new lawyer.

Chapter 3

How to Be a Good Client

A Key to Your Success

In my lifetime, I have had as clients for divorce proceedings doctors, dentists, my own personal lawyers, psychologists, plumbers, electricians, builders, accountants and every other type of worker, tradesman, and professional. They are all better in their field of expertise than I am. When I have sought their professional services and have been their client in their areas of expertise, I can't remember ever engaging them in arguments, yelling at them, hysterically crying over the phone to them, blaming them for all my problems, or seeing them as anything but potential solutions to whatever specific problem I've brought to them. And they don't typically do that with me. But, as hard as it might be to believe this, some divorce clients do exactly that.

Criminals who have lawyers, and so are officially clients of those attorneys, have very little to complain about. Most likely, in any instance, they've committed a crime and are guilty. They can only hope for the best deal available. It's different in the world of family law. There are two sides to the story, and both spouses likely have strong feelings about their own way of seeing things.

And as I say, I can't remember having one discussion in which I got into a heated argument with my doctor, psychologist, dentist, veterinarian, or other skilled professional about their prescribed course of action. In fact, I can't remember any discussions of my concerns I've had with them outside office visits. In the modern world, my access to them is typically limited, mostly by their staff, whom I often find to be very engaging and receptive to my problems.

In many people's minds, however, the exception to how all other professions work seems to be in the world of domestic law. To their way of thinking, it can even seem that divorce lawyers somehow make worse nearly all the problems that exist in their world. We domestic lawyers can take the brunt of their frustrations and anger, not only about their ex-husbands or wives, but about the legal system and virtually everything else that's going on in their lives. Clients even leave an attorney's office yelling and slamming doors if they're not getting their way in court. But that never makes things better.

This is not always how things go, but it does happen a lot. By the very nature of the business, domestic attorneys try to provide clients with a very clear and understandable service surrounded in a highly charged and emotional situation, all the time working within the complexities of domestic law.

Before we talk about ways in which you can maneuver well through the system without your lawyer either becoming utterly exasperated or infuriated with you, which is extremely detrimental to your outcomes, there are some clear duties we should lay out that the attorney owes to you.

What the Divorce Attorney Owes You

The Truth. From the initial meeting, your lawyer needs to tell you the truth. Sometimes the truth hurts and causes you to head to another attorney. If you search long enough, you can probably find some lawyer who will only tell you what you want to hear. If you do hear exactly what you want to hear, you're likely being misled. Attorneys can be sensitive to your issues, but they must be honest. If not, there will certainly come a point in time, either in mediation, trial, or the final settlement of your case, where you look at your lawyer and realized you've been deceived. There is a simple analogy: If you have a disease, you would probably appreciate the doctor telling you so truthfully in the first meeting, so you can both manage it as well as possible. You don't want false reassurances, hype, and empty hope. You want realistic assessments, plans, and solutions. Domestic lawyers owe you the same duty.

An Explanation. Not only do domestic attorneys owe you the truth, but we also owe you a thorough explanation of the process you will be going through. Good domestic attorneys should do this in the first meeting. Attorneys should tell you about the potential slowness and obstacles in your case. They should make it clear about the points of frustration you will experience while meandering your way through the legal system.

Quite frankly, no matter how hard we try, in the first meeting our advice simply does not always fully register and take hold. This will require attorneys to repeat on numerous occasions the same mantra over and over. We don't mind doing that, but at some point, we must do what we can to make sure it resonates with the client. That's our responsibility as lawyers.

For example, often in larger jurisdictions, you will get a notice in the mail stating that your case is appearing on the two-week calendar beginning on a specific Monday. However, this does not mean your case will be heard that Monday. It means that it will hopefully be heard sometime during that calendar period, depending on how many cases are before yours and how long they take. This needs to be communicated to you as the client. Fortunately, most judges will tell the attorneys exactly what day your case will be on. We will then let you know. However, cases often get postponed for a variety of reasons such as for an illness of an attorney or the judge, or the opposing counsel has a court time conflict, or there is a chance for settlement, or it could even be that both parties simply aren't ready to go to trial. The best we can do is inform you of when your case will be coming up and the likelihood that it will be heard then.

Lawyers have a responsibility to thoroughly explain to you the system and how it works so that you will understand what's coming down the line. We have a duty to at least explain the fundamental ins and outs of the law itself as it applies to your case. This should be done during the initial conference with you as client. However, since there can be information overload at an emotional time, attorneys don't expect a client to understand everything that's said in the initial conference. The process of divorce, particularly if it involves minor children, significant assets, claims for alimony, or a business can be very complicated. Nor do we expect you to completely understand everything even as the case rolls along. Good attorneys should review and explain the process to you perhaps several times over the months, in a rational and professional manner. It's what we do as a part of our service to you.

Respect. We owe you the duty of treating you respectfully. We should show you compassion for the situation you're going through. This doesn't mean we are the answer to all your problems. It does mean that you are entitled to be informed and told when your requests or demands are unrealistic and cannot be met. This includes the fact that virtually nothing can be done to solve a particular problem on a Friday night or over the weekend.

A Disclosure of Fees. You deserve reasonable billing. Divorce attorneys almost always bill by the hour. I'm often amazed at what people can perceive to be unreasonable. But most clients will be able to respect and understand that we are going to bill for the hours put into a case. This includes phone calls, meetings, and answering long e-mails. It also includes all the behind-the-scenes work that the system requires, such as document drafting, pleading, discovery, and interrogatories, which will be explained later. Also, it's important to remember that an attorney's staff time, particularly the important work of paralegals, is billable. The cost of copying documents and other "out of pocket" expenses can also be charged.

Attorney fees are found in many forms. Most lawyers will approach you with what is called a "retainer," which can run from inexpensive, if the case is not complicated and is usually around $2,500, to anywhere from $10,000 to $25,000, depending on your jurisdiction and the complexity of the case. A retainer is money that you give us up front to represent you. There's also a concept called "an earned fee" which allows us to deposit an entire fee that has been paid up front into our operating account. We will bill from day one against that deposited fee and if the fee exceeds what's needed, you may have the right to a refund.

Some attorneys will use a "flat fee" concept in which you pay a set amount for all services. This is generally seen in relatively simple cases. The flat fee can be advantageous, depending on the amount, for the lawyer. This is particularly true if the case can be resolved quickly, since flat fees are not returned to the client. It can also be a fee situation abused by a client, with the thought that it grants unlimited free rein to dominate the lawyer's time.

Diligence and Hard Work on Your Case. We owe you hard work and diligence in your case. We also owe you, in my opinion, the "big picture approach" to keep you from spending hundreds and thousands of dollars arguing over everything from the Tupperware, pick-up and drop-off places for visitation, and other issues that should clearly be resolved by the adults you are. If we, as your lawyers, feed into that mentality, not only will the process be extremely frustrating, but it will become far more expensive than it needs to be. I have always been "a big picture lawyer." The frustration of receiving letters or listings from other lawyers proposing division of shoes, clothing, photographs, athletic equipment, vacuum cleaners, and dishware is stifling. Bringing to the attention of your attorney anything but the most valuable items in your household will bog down the process and will lead to incredible aggravation and expense.

Reasonable Communication. We owe you a return phone call within a reasonable length of time. Every message left at the office of a physician, psychologist, dentist, or any other professional generally gets returned within a day or two. You can reasonably expect this.

At most professional offices, it's generally a staff member who returns a call, unless it really is something the lead professional needs to address. It's like trying to talk to a physician. Doctors do not always have the time to get on the phone and discuss your problems in detail every time you may call their office. Rather the physician's office staff will call back or arrange to set up an appointment. If there is a true emergency, you will get a message to call 911. Domestic lawyers don't have that luxury. There is no 911 for domestic law emergencies. When a client calls with what they perceive to be an urgent problem, we, unlike almost any other profession, owe you a personal call back. If it is not an emergency, most likely you will hear from the staff. But getting a reasonable response to your communication should be expected. In your initial meeting with your attorney, discuss the communication policy so there is no confusion. But you, as a client, must also have a reasonable communication outlook, and that's covered in the next section.

Best Effort. Finally, in the end we owe you our best effort. We do not owe you the result necessarily that you expected or even hoped for, but we owe you the preparation, effort and passion it takes to potentially get that result or to come as close as we can.

Your Responsibilities as a Client

Responsibility needs to be a two-way street. As a client, you also have a responsibility, just like any patient who has been given a diagnosis and needs to follow a prescribed plan for a cure, as well as adhering to the instructions on how to do it. Domestic lawyers are no exception. So here are the rules that you should follow if you want to maintain a good relationship with your divorce lawyer. They are simple and properly humane expectations. Following these rules will help your lawyer to like you instead of merely representing you. And that always helps, because we're only human. These rules will help you survive the travails of your case without damaging everybody's nerves, resolve, family life, or personal happiness.

Don't Over Shop for Lawyers. Certainly, you need to find an attorney who is a good fit. That's a given, and it's the whole purpose of the previous section. But there are some clients who pretend to interview many lawyers, or "shop lawyers," not to find a good fit, but rather for the purpose of ensuring that the soon-to-be ex-spouse will not be able to hire any of them for their side of the case. Even a first meeting with a lawyer makes it difficult for the other spouse to get an appointment, due to potential conflicts This is particularly true in smaller communities where the number of domestic attorneys might be limited. Some spouses think it's a clever tactic, but it will only hurt in the end. Good lawyers work well with their peers, and these top notch attorneys often get your case resolved much more efficiently and inexpensively. Such lawyers are reluctant to represent a "shopper" who is already pulling underhanded, dirty tricks.

For the lawyer it is in fact a form of cheating, if you're simply going around town having chats with lawyers you don't want to see oppose you. That has never made much sense to me, but it does cost good lawyers business, and it costs the shopper a more honest and humane approach to the case. If this happens, the other spouse will usually go out of town for representation. He or she might then find a stronger lawyer or possibly hire someone who will aggravate the hell out of your case, which will ultimately cost you a lot more money. Shopping lawyers for this reason is not a good strategy. You're free to interview a few attorneys and hire the one you are most comfortable with. However, if your purpose is to simply eliminate other local lawyers from your spouse's search, it will be counterproductive in the end.

Don't Think You Own the Attorney. This really shouldn't have to be said, but when you pay an attorney, you don't then "own" that person in any way. I've had that phrase said to me on several occasions and am simply astounded by it. It doesn't work even as jocular hyperbole. You pay professionals to do the best job they can do for you. There is indeed a distinctive client relationship, but by no means do you "own" that attorney for any duration of time at all. I would never say such a thing to any professional in my life, like those who have built my homes or have provided any type of expert service for me in the past. It's disrespectful, even if said in jest, and only serves to diminish you in the eyes of the lawyer and his or her staff. You can take ownership of yourself, and of the situation, but never of the professionals helping you.

Lawyers are Sensitive Listeners, But They are Not Therapists. A lawyer is not your therapist, psychologist, counselor, or spiritual advisor. We're not qualified to diagnose disorders, nor can we provide professional psychological therapy. Based on years of experience seeing all types of clients, attorneys can certainly listen and perhaps give some comfort or broad advice. But attorneys do not have the resolution, skill sets, or training to address every emotional up and down you will go through during a divorce. There are plenty of good psychologists and counselors, priests and pastors, as well as close friends and family you can confide in through that process. We attorneys can't solve your psychological problems, and we certainly can't solve your spouse's. We may try to help with your emotions, but we can't reliably bring you down from the intense and unpleasant agitation or anger that divorces often create.

Attorneys are also fellow human beings and can only do the best they can. We also cost far more per hour than a friend, or about the same as a psychologist or therapist who will be far better trained to manage major emotional issues. So, try to remember to turn to them for the things on which we aren't your best option. You should, however, always expect answers to your legal questions, and in a properly sensitive manner, from your lawyer.

Respect the Staff. Payment of a retainer fee does not allow anyone to be disrespectful, mean, hardhearted, or cruel to the lawyer's staff. Staff members are simply there to work for you, and if necessary, to convey your frustrations to your lawyer. They are not there to be demeaned or threatened. Nor do they tend to take kindly to harsh criticism of their employer, the attorney on your case. They will often naturally become defensive. If a client complains too much, the staff will simply walk into their employer's office with word of what's happened. This never puts a client in a good light or helps their case. If you as a client have a legitimate complaint and state it in an adult, civilized, rational, and thoughtful manner, it can help with things. And most likely, the response you receive will be in the same tone. When any client lashes out at an attorney's staff in an angry manner, it produces unwanted negative consequences, as in most of life.

Schedule Your Appointments. The lawyer's office is no different than a doctor, dentist, veterinarian, or any other professional practice. You simply can't arrive unannounced and sit in the waiting room until your needs are met. In our work, despite the "By Appointment Only" sign we hang on our door, too many potential and current clients just show up at the office unannounced. That's certainly OK for dropping off some required documents to the receptionist or paralegal, but not to see the attorney immediately. The office is usually serving a lot of other people with equally pressing problems.

The lawyer's office is neither a legal emergency room, nor a place where you can simply drop in any time you have a problem. Just call and make an appointment. On occasion, you can get an time for your visit quickly. Most offices are good at trying to fit you in. Once you have an appointment, you will then have the full attention of your attorney. You also need to understand that if you have a good and popular lawyer, such a professional is often called to court at the last minute, or a judge may need to talk to them about something. Despite their best efforts, attorneys will sometimes simply be late to your appointment or will have to change it because the court has altered his or her schedule. Try to be flexible in such matters. We will certainly try to be as flexible as we can with you. And of course, attorneys can also get sick and may have to miss a day or two of work. It's an obvious fact of life, but anyone can forget such things in times of distress.

Have Reasonable Expectations. Don't believe everything you hear on the street about a lawyer. There's no domestic lawyer on earth who has had a smooth and untroubled relationship with every client represented. By its very nature, divorce often seems like a no-win proposition, particularly to a client who thinks they deserve everything. Most of the time, you will emerge from a divorce case moderately unhappy but not miserable. If you expect the world, you'll simply not get it. That's fiction, no matter how much an attorney says they'll fight for you and win.

Call Only Once Per Day at Most. The more demanding and abrasive a client is, the more the attorney's office will dread their calls. Even cordial clients can overdo phone contact from nervous worry. One call per day will do. Phoning back six or seven times because your call has not been returned immediately gets you little love, or a heightened inclination to quickly return your calls. Most lawyers will inevitably return a call within a reasonable time, often before the end of the day. There are hundreds of other phone calls, court proceedings, and meetings with other clients that can make it difficult to respond to a telephoned problem immediately.

Understand the Office Communications Policy. You'd be amazed at the many clients I give my personal cell phone number to. Most attorneys will not do this, for understandable reasons. But some do. I do so for the purpose of allowing clients to reach me after hours when they can't get me during the day, and text me information that I might need. But please note, an attorney giving out a personal phone number to a client is not providing an open invitation for frequent calls throughout the weekend, or at dinner time. Just like anybody, we are need some type of free time. It helps us to be refreshed and ready to be at our best for your case.

My own personal policy is that I will inevitably return a call within a day. My workday extends from around 7:30 in the morning until 8 at night, Monday through Friday. After 5:00pm, at the end of my appointments, you can often expect a return call. Some people think I'm crazy to have this long a schedule. Many attorneys do consider the job an 8 to 5, Monday to Friday commitment only, and hold the line with those boundaries. That doesn't mean they're slackers or less engaged lawyers. We simply have different professional rhythms or ideas about work. The key thing is to discuss your phone/contact expectations with your attorney up front, so there is no confusion. And please follow the guidelines of your attorney's policies.

Respect is Reciprocal. A good client is the best client. This is the one who treats all members of the legal office with respect, has a sense of humor, handles the process well, does not demand the world, and doesn't expect a lawyer to resolve every problem that may have been created through a lifetime of frustrating experiences. While an attorney can certainly be empathetic, we are not superheroes who can make every problem you have disappear.

In short, you should treat your lawyer the same way you would treat a good but casual friend. Share a joke, be friendly, be kind, apologize if you make a mistake, and they will likely respond in the same way. This works in every profession.

Confusing and Multiple Long E-mails Don't Work. Do not text or e-mail incessantly. If you have something important to communicate to the attorney's office, please do so as efficiently as you can. Try to get your thoughts together in one e-mail or text. Put them in a brief, clearly readable form. Expecting someone to read long multiple diatribes or convoluted stories that come in four or five different formats throughout the day not only costs you billable time but frustrates your attorney and staff immeasurably. You might be surprised how often this happens. When you discipline your communications with your lawyer, things go much better.

Listen Honestly to Your Attorney. Finally, you have a responsibility to listen honestly to your attorney and with an open mind. Once you have asked a question and the lawyer has answered, it does you no good to repeat the same question that's been answered, over and over. Some people simply cannot take for an answer "no," or "it doesn't work that way," or "the law won't allow for that". These emotionally deaf clients often repeat themselves time and again hoping for a different answer. Once you have asked a question and have an answer, go to a different issue. If you need to, write it all down, but do your best not to ask it again. And above all, please don't always expect a simple, straightforward answer to every question. The law is complex. Life is messy. This is why e-mail has become so ineffective in dealing with lawyers. To avoid a phone call that may not be returned, many clients send long e-mails with numerous questions that no lawyer in his or her right mind would answer in writing. The reason is that there is often no one "right" or "wrong" answer, and in a world where surprises lurk, no good lawyer would commit themselves in advance and in writing to one. Lawyers cannot guarantee anything except their own hard work and best efforts. Family law just doesn't work that way.

Closing Thoughts on the Client-Attorney Relationship

In closing, if both you and your lawyer follow these simple rules, you will have an amicable and cordial process. Your lawyer's office may become a refuge for you because your lawyer and the office staff will grow to like you and enjoy seeing you come in. Lawyers talk, and judges do too. If someone creates a nuisance and is difficult to work with, especially if they have fired lawyer after lawyer in dissatisfaction, they will become known around the courthouse as "a problem client." And this helps only the other side. It's exceedingly easy not to become one of these people. In the end, a good working relationship arises from a combination of duties, both on the one side as a lawyer and on the other as a client—to respect each other, do a good job, and work hard at your own part of the relationship. If an client-attorney partnership is not at this level, then it's probably a good time to end it on an amicable basis.

Chapter 4

How the Law Works in Divorce

There are Some Rules

In my practice, I often get e-mails from clients asking me specific legal questions, expecting that I'll respond with quick specific answers. That will never happen, except if the question is an exceedingly easy one. The fact is that family law has a lot of gray areas. Most often, the answers are not black or white, but somewhere in the range of other color spectrums.

If a lawyer responds with what he or she feels is a definitive answer, there is a possibility they're simply catering to you and not telling the complete truth. Questions need to be answered clearly, with forthright honesty, and with compassion, but promises cannot often be made. Remember, if you have a smart lawyer, he or she will probably not reply to an email on the law or on likely outcomes with a definitive response in writing. That sort of thing can make the attorney vulnerable to potential lawsuits and an accusation that things didn't go as promised. Quite frankly, conversations will likely be more open in person. The fact is that there is often no definitive answer to many questions, only guidelines within which a lawyer can be creative.

Just because the law has been interpreted in a certain case or an issue has been decided in a certain way in the past does not mean that your lawyer can't argue something different to the court. A good attorney can even ask for a dramatic change in the judge's use of past laws that have accrued over the years but are in dire need of amendment. That's why the law is an ever-evolving process, and for lawyers who evolve with it, it's endlessly interesting.

Every state is different in the details of domestic law. The one major difference you often hear about is that some states are "Community Property States" while others are "Equitable Distribution States." We will talk more about this in our chapter on property. But in all states, the law originates from three definitive sources. This chapter may read a little like a freshman college law text, but it's important that you understand some of these differences. It will help you appreciate what's happening as you progress through the stages of your case, and to communicate better with your attorney on these issues. There are several sources of the law.

Source of Domestic & Family Laws - Statutory Laws

All states have laws that have been enacted by mandate of the general assembly or state legislature—these are of course the law-making bodies of state-level elected officials. These laws appear in what are normally called "General or State Statutes." Statutes are supposed to be strictly followed. In most states, there is also what's called a "family law counsel" that's been formed to assist the legislature, or there are "family law lawyers" who have come together to influence legislators to pass sensible laws that we can rationally apply to the domestic situations we deal with on a daily basis.

In my fifteenth year of practicing law, I had the pleasure of serving on the North Carolina Bar Association Family Law Counsel, and for two years I learned not only a tremendous amount of law, but also what each family lawyer was dealing with across the state. In addition, I learned how the best ideas are taken to local legislators to be codified in the General Statutes of any particular state. This is a meticulous and sometimes harrowing process. I then had the honor of serving on the Family Law Counsel for a second time, perhaps because I have been involved in a body of appellate law cases, some of which I've lost and some of which I've won.

What the General Assembly has voted on and the Governor has signed, in fact, becomes the law. And it is that law whose dictates we must follow. Luckily, this law has often been produced from the State Bar Association's recommendations. This might be one of the few situations where lobbying efforts in politics have positive results. The laws generally, but not always, make sense by the time they are recorded into the books of the General Statutes. But regardless of whether it makes sense or not, it's now ordained to be followed by family lawyers. Certainly, not all States agree on everything. We can discuss examples of the coordination of efforts in domestic law, one that results in agreement between the States, and one where there is little agreement between the States.

An Example of Agreements Between the States: The Uniform Child Custody Act

The Act. The first example is the Uniform Child Custody Jurisdiction Act. It's the result of intensive work by good lawyers. In these statutory provisions there are laws that are applied in every child custody case and are universal throughout the country. If there are minor children involved with a divorce, your lawyer will make efforts to explain it all to you. We will discuss this a little later in this book regarding one of the crucial issues of family law: child custody.

Another example is the Uniform Reciprocal Enforcement of Support Act. This law basically allows you to enforce a support obligation from an ex-spouse who owes you support. This is true even if they have lodged themselves in another state, often to avoid support obligations. Sooner or later, they will be tracked down and the laws will be enforced. To say this is a slow process is a vast understatement, but the laws are in place.

An Example of Little Agreement Between States: Home-Wrecker Laws

An example of where the states have no consensus whatsoever are the laws on suing a third-party who has had either sexual relations with a spouse or "lured your spouse away from your relationship." The idea here is that somebody has maliciously interfered with a marital relationship and they should be punished. These are often called "homewrecker laws." The two primary home-wrecker laws are "Alienation of Affection," and "Criminal Conversation". While the innocent spouse may feel such laws are highly relevant in their case of a spouse sleeping around or having a prolonged affair, most states have done away with such laws.

Many people view these ideas as left-over concepts from the distant past when wives were often seen as personal "property" that could be stolen, and the husband suffers a lack of conjugal relations due to the intervention of a third party. Long ago in these situations the men would duel it out with swords or pistols. The 2021 movie, the "Last Duel" depicts a true fourteenth century event in France that involved accusations of infidelity. After dueling was banned, lawsuits became more popular, but initially they were almost always filed against another man who was said to have stolen the wife. Now, of course, either gender can file.

There are only a few remaining states that have homewrecker laws to varying degrees. These include Hawaii, Mississippi, New Mexico, South Dakota, Utah, and North Carolina. North Carolina and Mississippi are where most of the homewrecker cases are still filed, although there are movements in all the states still having these laws to abolish them. One can certainly debate the logic of such laws in the modern world. Objections to removing a homewrecker law often focus on the moral component; however, there is also an overlooked economic argument that can be made to keep these laws, almost as with a wrongful death case. After all, infidelity creates a shared and contributory negligence by the third-party. And in this case, it contributes to the "death of a marriage." As in a wrongful death case involving a guilty or liable party, there are similar economic benefits each party provides the marriage that are now lost by the contributory actions of another. Regardless of how we view them, we do need to cover these laws, particularly since both of us as authors work extensively in states that have them.

Alienation of Affection. "Alienation of Affection" by its own terms is obvious on its face, making it easy to understand. You first prove that there was a true love and affection between husband and wife. You then often must prove that a third-party entered the scene, was able to attract the affections of the spouse and "lure" them away from the marriage. This is extremely difficult to prove, because in every alienation of affection case we have encountered, the defense is that an unhappy marriage existed before the third-party ever entered. None of us has a perfect marriage, and sometimes an affair is understood and forgiven. Alienation of affection arises when the third-party relationship is the procuring cause, but not a singular cause that brings a marriage to an end.

Criminal Conversation. The second term is "criminal conversation." This simply means that someone else had sex with your husband or wife. The term "criminal conversation" is at best ludicrous. We have yet to find the definitive origin of the phrase. Whoever came up with it was probably living in long ago, when it wasn't acceptable to say "sex" in public, so the term "conversation" was used instead. Essentially, criminal conversation is a civil claim for the act of "adultery," regardless as to whether it had an impact on the marriage ending or not. Criminal conversation torts were developed when adultery was illegal. A smart lawyer can often add to the allegation by tacking on an "intentional infliction of emotional distress" claim and punitive damages claim.

People read headlines about these cases all the time and think this is a viable option for pushing their own case to a successful conclusion. The large verdicts in these cases are mostly won when the other party does not even bother to appear, or when in a very aggravated situation a jury finds a large amount of money should be warranted against a third-party for their actions. More often these days, such claims are used primarily as a tactic to move the opposing party to think more seriously about settling.

A Note on Same-Sex Marriages

Although we speak throughout this book about marriage in a husband and wife context, we are sensitive to the issue of same-sex marriages. At one time, even recently, some states had different rules regarding same-sex marriages. This is important since marriages and divorces are covered by state laws, not federal law. Many of these rules were even set into the constitutions of the different states. More recently, and really since 2015 with an important U.S. Supreme Court decision (*Obergefell v. Hodges*), many states have started to change their constitutional bans on same-sex marriages and have extended civil marriage unions to same-sex couples. In 2022, the *Respect for Marriage Act* was passed with bipartisan support, which legally protects both same-sex marriages and racially mixed marriages from being banned by state laws. So, in general, any existing state constitutional prohibitions against same-sex marriages are currently not enforceable.

The bottom line is that since same-sex marriages are currently recognized in all states within the U.S., the process of divorce and the issues discussed in this book are as equally applicable to these marriages as to heterosexual unions. Although research is scarce, the current evidence from many countries including the U.S., is that divorce rates among same-sex marriages are about the same, or perhaps a little higher, than different-gender marriages. However, the divorce rates appear to be rising much faster among same-sex couples. Also, research indicates that married female couples are more likely to initiate a dissolution process than married gay men. Regardless, the same issues exist, such as personal pain and emotional distress, financial concerns, child and custody issues, spousal support, and property settlement. This is now the same for all types of marriage unions regardless of gender orientation. Both the authors of this book have worked on cases related to the dissolution of same-sex marriages.

Common Law Marriages and Divorce

Simply put, common law marriages are legal marriages without an official marriage license or marriage certificate. There is an ancient history of common-law marriages where couples took up residence together and held themselves out to be married. Originally, almost all the states in the U.S. allowed for such marriages, many times recognizing that in very poor rural areas or in the large expanses of the Wild West, couples might not physically be able to get to a pastor, priest, or official county office, and it was felt that if children were involved, they would benefit from growing up in the context of a legal marriage. However, most states have now eliminated common law marriage, with South Carolina and Alabama abolishing them most recently. As of the writing of this book, there are only eight states (Colorado, Iowa, Kansas, Montana, Rhode Island, Oklahoma, and Texas) along with the District of Columbia that recognize common law marriage in some form. A couple of federally recognized tribes also recognize these marriages. Utah and New Hampshire legally recognize common law marriages under only very limited circumstances.

Common law marriages, when and where recognized, however, do not occur simply by cohabitating for a long period of time. In general, there are five basic requirements. These five requirements are: (a) Capacity (legal age and a mental capacity to consent), (b) Agreement (written or oral evidence of an agreement to be married; not just a promise to be married in the future), (c) Cohabitation (living together continuously and openly as spouses, with some states requiring a stated minimum amount of time), (d) Holding Out (this means the couple presents themselves to others as being married, not as girlfriend or boyfriend, but rather as husband and wife—so, a common law marriage cannot be a secret), and (e) Reputation (that the community, including other family members, views the couple as married, and not just as sleeping together). These elements are often proven (or disproven) by documents, such as filing a married tax return, changing to a common name, applying for loans as a married couple, and so on.

While common law marriages are somewhat rare, it's important to realize that a couple involved in a common law marriage must go through the same legal divorce process as any other married couple. They cannot obtain a "common law divorce" by simply moving apart. The exact same issues of separation requirements, filing a petition for divorce, property division, child custody and support, and spousal support apply to a common law marriage. What is often seen, however, is that a divorcing partner in a common law marriage might claim they really weren't legally married in the first place, if it impacts property division or spousal support. In these cases, the family law attorney may need to prove a couple was or was not married through a common law process, in addition to normal divorce proceedings.

Source of Domestic & Family Laws - Case Law

After reading through the Statutory Law section, you might think that state laws tell domestic lawyers exactly what they are to do and that's the end of it. But you would be wrong. There are appellate courts in every state. Throughout the year, despite the best efforts of the various legislatures and the Family Law Councils that have debated, pondered over, and attempted to create a uniform system of laws to follow, each case will be decided on its own merits and will present a different fact situation. Creative lawyers do not follow every bit of language in the General Statutes. No matter how hard our politicians may try, seemingly unambiguous statutory law will always be open to interpretation, and so with almost every domestic case of any import the lawyer will have taken the General Statute and put their own spin on it. While these Statutes provide a framework, they don't determine everything. A trial judge may or may not agree with the lawyer's interpretation. And if there is an appeal, it will go to the state's appellate courts.

In most states there are two levels for appeal, the Court of Appeals and the Supreme Court (which rarely sees domestic cases). Most disputed domestic cases are decided at one panel or another of the Court of Appeals. These courts all sit in separate panels and have a bad habit in every state of not following what the other panel is doing and instead sending out to trial and domestic lawyers varying interpretations of what they think the law is. Accordingly, we're sometimes left with conflicting decisions based on a case that may or may not be close to the situation we're dealing with now. There are many appellate court decisions in states that are just contradictory. It's part of the attorney's job to navigate these differences.

As lawyers, we tend to seize on case law that supports our position, which often involves an interpretation of whatever the General Statute or a particular past decision has attempted to say, and we as lawyers are entitled to argue it. Judges, in turn, can agree or disagree with our argument. When judges disagree, this, in turn, can often lead to more appeals.

It is our case law that produces either consistent or inconsistent laws that we have to deal with on a trial-by-trial basis in family law. Accordingly, domestic lawyers, just as other lawyers in almost every other aspect of law, are left with a dizzying mix of statutory and case laws. These often conflict and leave us in a lot of gray areas. So, you, as a client, can understand that there's a reason lawyers can't give you a definitive answer to some of your questions.

The Trial Court

As you've seen above, the trial court and the lawyers who appear before it are supposed to follow either the statutory law that's set out or the history of how case law has interpreted it. Sometimes, we don't agree with the case law that's interpreted the statutory law, and on occasion we don't all agree with the statutory law. Further, in most states, you can cite many conflicting decisions from the Appellate Courts. It's a tangle.

Family law attorneys often joke that there's a second set of rules in domestic court, informally called "the Domestic Court Rules." Lawyers who dare to venture into the domestic court find themselves in a world they may never have thought existed. It's different from civil litigation, criminal law, and business cases that lawyers deal with in other courts. Quite frankly, domestic attorneys will often find that normal evidentiary rules don't necessarily apply. They will discover that often the comments between counsel and in cross-examination are not in the same tone or done in accord with the procedural processes that exist in the other areas of law.

To a vast majority of clients, your divorce case may be the only time you're ever involved in litigation. And for most people, it's the one type of litigation that involves a complex mix of personal assets combined with incredible and conflicting emotions. This is a warning to clients going through a divorce who try to use attorneys who work in many different fields of law, without focusing just on domestic law. To be adept in domestic court, the attorney needs to know aspects of all areas of law, including real estate, bankruptcy, and in many cases large scale business valuations, tax law, and investment law. And, in addition, a domestic attorney needs to bring all this knowledge into a clear focus for their domestic cases. Only the toughest, and dare I say, the craziest, survive in this field. The very best domestic lawyers know their craft, work hard on your case, tell the truth, and seek to bring it all to a fair conclusion.

Most domestic lawyers often deal with large estates, businesses, investments, and pensions that far exceed the monetary awards that might result in normal civil litigation. Having said all this, we need to cover some very basic terms that should apply nationally from state-to-state. We outline here only the basics, because your own domestic lawyer will bear the responsibility of educating you to the difficulties of your case in your state. But it's always good to understand the basics.

First, let's work through some concepts. As always, different states have somewhat different rules, at least in the details. This section only provides the most general guidance. You always need to talk to your attorney about the specific processes and time periods in your state.

No Fault Divorce: All states have enacted some versions of no-fault divorce laws, although different states will put their own spin on the specifics of their no-fault laws.

Separation Requirements. Most states require you to be separated for a period prior to getting a no-fault divorce. This time of separation differs from state to state but is typically 6 months to a year. At the time of writing this book, only six states do not allow for a legally filed separation. In Delaware, Florida, Georgia, Mississippi, Pennsylvania and Texas, you can't file for a legal separation, but rather need to file directly for divorce. Some states require a longer separation period if children are involved. In some states, after separating for a year, the couple needs to file for divorce or reconcile, while in other states you can remain separated and never divorce. The bottom line is that each state looks at separation differently. Learn your state's rules.

Residency Requirements. To file for a divorce in a particular state, you also generally need to meet a residency requirement in that state. These requirements are established so spouses don't shop states to file in. They vary by state. Only a few states, like Alaska, South Dakota and Washington don't have fixed residency requirements (or they actually have something like one, but it's not well defined). In North Carolina and many other states, at least one spouse must reside in the state for 6 months. Nevada simply requires a personal presence, and not a legal residency for any duration to file for separation, and only 6 weeks of residency to file for divorce. States also have different rules when only one spouse lives in the state. Some states, such as California, also have residency requirements at the county level.

If the two spouses legally reside in different states, they can each apply for divorce in their state of residency, but, normally, once the first state issues a decree, then the filing in the other state becomes invalid. For members of the armed forces, there are even some different residency requirements. You need to check with your attorney regarding residency requirements or at least check the law on the web before embarking on the process.

Once you've satisfied both the separation requirement and residency requirement for your state, if there is one, you're entitled to file for divorce. The divorce itself is probably the simplest part of the process. Sometime after you have met the requirements that apply in your state, you will simply walk into a court and, in most cases, say "We have been separated for the required duration, and it's time to divorce us." If you can prove that you've lived separate from your spouse for the designated time and you are a resident, if required, which 99% of the time you can, you will get divorced. The judges will basically take you at your word. In most cases, there is no opposition to divorce.

When to Bring a Claim for Divorce. Except in the simplest of cases, though, the term "divorce" often has little to do with your case from the attorney's perspective. Divorce is a legal action that will take place toward the end of your case. But the legal granting of divorce may have little impact on the entire process. This is because there's inevitably property that must be dealt with, as well as support issues, and possibly children. Divorce can happen well before the property division is decided. We've been many cases where the parties were divorced, remarried to others, and have children with new spouses and the courts were still deciding on the property settlements from the first marriage. This is very stressful, and quite frankly, not overly humane to all the parties involved. But it can happen if you don't work to see that it doesn't.

One important warning: Don't ever allow yourself to get divorced without bringing up in legal form, or at least alleging, before the divorce is granted, the areas of the things you want, especially with the division of assets and payment of support in the form of assets or money. Most states will bar these claims later if you divorce without first bringing a claim for equitable distribution/property division or spousal support. It must be brought before the divorce decree.

What Does "Separation" Actually Mean?

Above, we spoke of "separation," but we need to fine-tune this definition a little. There is a common misconception throughout much of the general population as to exactly what separation in this context means. It can signify many different things to the average person, but there are some important types of separation that need to be understood.

Legal Separation: As mentioned above, most states allow for a "legal separation." The easiest way to explain a legal separation is this: You and your spouse have either voluntarily agreed to enter into a legally notarized separation agreement, which can be as simple as saying you're legally separated, and it will hold your other various issues open for future litigation.

You can also sign a "separation and property settlement agreement" that deals with your issues of not only separation from each other but how you want to divide your assets and the payment of alimony or spousal support for the designated spouse.

However, you do not include child custody and support provisions in a separation and property settlement agreement. Any child custody and support arrangement you've agreed on at this stage is simply a personal agreement between you and your spouse and, while persuasive, it's not binding on the court. Your decision can be a private contract on dividing your assets and spousal support. But it is not simply a private matter in child custody and child support cases.

If you can work out child custody and support issues on your own, however, that's great. Time and money and lots of emotional stress can be saved. But if you're going to include child custody and support in your agreement, you will need to have it placed into a court order signed by a judge. That is easy to do, and this should be done in every case, otherwise you may find yourself in a situation somewhere down the line where you are being sued for custody, even though you thought you had laid that issue to rest in your separation agreement.

There are, in some states, laws that allow you to go into court and ask the court to "legally separate" you, regardless of what your spouse thinks. This sometimes requires a showing of fault from one spouse. Taking this approach as an individual action will often aggravate the situation. In our opinion, it's better to work out your differences and enter, at the very least, a mutually agreed legal separation that allows you to move on with your life.

Physical Separation: In many states physical separation has become much more important and has negated the immediate need of a legal separation agreement, at least for purposes of moving toward a final divorce. In most states, physical separation is a form of legal separation. It starts the clock on when you can get divorced, and in many states (but not all), it will be a cut-off point in deciding whether property acquired after this date is marital or separate. In these states, simply living physically separated from your spouse is the key. Physically separating does not mean you are sleeping in one bedroom in your house and your spouse is sleeping in the other, and you're not talking. Unfortunately, that describes many marriages, but it's not generally considered physical separation in the relevant sense.

Physical separation will require two things—one spouse moving out of the marital home, and actions by either one or both spouses that indicate they intend to separate legally. This intent is often shown by getting separate bank accounts, separate insurance, and other actions. Another thing needs to be clear: As long as you don't move back in with each other during the time that's required to obtain your divorce, your period of separation will not be disrupted by dating or even occasional acts of sexual intercourse with your now separated spouse. I find those cases few and far between. But they do emerge from time to time.

Note that many married couples become physically separated but still retain common family medical insurance. With the current cost of medical insurance, sharing this cost is obviously prudent. However, you need to be careful. Different medical plans have different rules about coverage of spouses when they are technically separated. Also, in some states, staying on the same insurance might indicate an intent not to separate. Check this with your attorney.

Can I Live in the Same House When Separated?

Sometimes people wonder if they can still live under the same roof when separated. This often happens for two reasons—for sharing expenses or from believing it's better for the children. The impact of living under the same roof really depends on both the emotional state you and your ex-spouse are in, and how the arrangement is set up. As previously discussed, there are several states, such as Florida, that don't recognize a separation—you either file for divorce or stay married. So, in these states, the issue is irrelevant once you file the petition for divorce. You can certainly move out and be physically separated for your own mental and physical wellbeing, or you can stay under the same roof. Filing for divorce basically states that the marriage is irretrievably broken and there's no chance of reconciling.

Most states have a legal separation process where you file a petition with the court and the court subsequently issues a legal document that sanctions the separation. In these cases, you can generally stay under the same roof; but, you probably should try to keep separate finances. This is particularly important if issues arise regarding property acquired after the date of separation. Since legal separation provides certain protections, essentially living under the same roof while legally separated is like living under the same roof while divorced. It's probably not a good idea but is generally legal.

As we've mentioned, many states recognize physical separation as a form of required separation, without the need to file a separation petition with the court. Physical separation counts toward the time specified to obtain a divorce, and in some states, is a defining date for property issues. In these states, without obtaining a legal separation, it's more difficult to live under the same roof, since the whole idea of a physical separation is to be bodily, spatially separated in a new and distinctive way. Some states, such as North Carolina, tend to be strict on this; however, other states do allow for a "separation under the same roof." In these cases, you will need to document that you remain physically separate while under the same roof. This certainly would involve proving you live in separate bedrooms, have separate finances and bank accounts, have reduced shared activities or family outings, and that you are now paying for separate car insurance, shopping separately, doing your own laundry, telling friends and family about the arrangement, and if purchasing any assets, then they are under your name only. If you are thinking about divorce and/or separation and want to continue living under the same roof for financial or child stability reasons, talk to your attorney about the laws, as well as the best way to document the separation.

Am I Staying Separated Too Long?

This is a very hard question. In many cases, couples will think about a trial separation, with the hope of possibly reconciling. In other examples, separated couples will act like they've been divorced for years, without ever filing for the final divorce. And in yet different cases, couples know definitely they want to divorce, and so they separate only for the minimum time required by their state before divorcing. The motivations for the length of separation are many and varied.

In theory, a separation is generally thought of as a trial peri-od. This is exactly why most states have a defined length of time you need to be separated prior to getting a divorce. They want people to consider divorce carefully, rather than quickly jumping into it every time something goes wrong in a marriage. This is understandable. Some states, however, have an upper time limit for separation. After this, you either reconcile or divorce.

Generally, the time in a separation is determined by the course of events, how long it takes to settle property, the time before a mediation date can be set up, the complexity of spousal or child support, and the personal desires of the parties involved. However, from our experience, separations in some cases can last far too long. This generally occurs for one of two reasons.

First, the separating couples are just afraid of taking the final step. Divorce sounds like, and is, a final decree, while separation doesn't seem quite as permanent. Some couples simply seem to live more comfortably under a separation agreement due to this fear of finality. However, this can interfere with the ability of the parties to buy property in their own name, get credit, find meaningful future relationships, and generally move ahead with their lives.

A second, more serious reason we see for extending separation too long is when one party has been in a controlling marriage, is timid, insecure, and maybe even afraid. In these cases, the more dominant partner might be in their own apartment, buying new cars and clothing, going on vacations and dating, while financially maintaining the less dominant partner. However, this maintenance is almost always far less than what the divorce would deliver in terms of alimony, child support, and the separation of marital property. In these cases, the dominant partner will gladly let the separation continue as long as they can. It's to their financial advantage, and they might even sound nice about it. The reason the less dominant partner doesn't just end it and file the divorce petition is almost always the same: They're afraid of what the dominating spouse will do. They've spent their whole marriage trying to keep the dominate spouse from getting angry, and it's hard to change that thought process even when separated. If you find yourself in this position, you really need to listen to your friends and family, and what they have to say. In these cases, filing a divorce petition will at least get things moving toward a better situation.

Separation and Divorce

Whatever the separation requirement is in your state—a year, six months, or whatever, once you do separate, the clock begins to run for when you can file for divorce. There is really nothing that can stop it in most states. After the residency and separation requirements are met, divorce is inevitable if one or the other party formally files for it. This is true whether the other spouse likes it or not. Our advice is to simply find a way to physically separate, within the rules above, and then the clock starts ticking.

In some states, assets and property that you have already acquired, meaning the assets that existed at the date of physical separation, will be divided with the physical date of separation as the line of demarcation, or as I call it, the line in the sand. But this is not always true. When it comes to property, different states can use different valuation dates, or dates that define whether property is separate or marital. Some states use the date of filing the petition for divorce as the cut-off date to define marital property. Other states might use filing for legal separation, not just physically moving out, as the cut-off point for defining whether property purchased after that date is marital or separate. There are many cases, for example, where one spouse received significant assets after physical separation (such as winning a lottery or a large bonus from work), but the courts still viewed these funds as marital property, since in that state there were different cut-off dates for purposes of property assignment.

Understanding the key cut-off date in your state for defining separate and marital property is important. You need to have this discussion with your attorney early in the process so there are no surprises later. States can differ dramatically on rules regarding property.

You also need to understand that the events that occur between your physical separation (or key cut-off date in your state) and the date you divide your assets are important, particularly in equitable distribution states. Although these issues have become muddled over the course of years by appellate decisions, in most states the only thing that should be subject to division after your date of separation/cut-off-date would be what is generally called the "passive increase or decreases" of the value of your assets, as well as payments made to preserve the estate. Much more about this will be discussed in our chapter on property.

In most states, once you are physically separated from your spouse, you're free to move on with your life. That means you can date, have sex, swing from the rafters, get drunk, hang out at bars, or do anything you feel is necessary to celebrate your freedom from a long-term marriage. This doesn't mean, however, that you should rush out and do it. If, in fact, you move in with or start dating a lover shortly after the physical date of separation, that can be used as evidence that an affair was going on before. Inappropriate actions, even after the date of separation, can also be brought up in child custody hearings. Just don't be stupid. Of course, that's generally a wise rule for life in any case, wholly apart from issues of marriage and divorce. It might make for a nice refrigerator magnet or tattoo, placed where you can easily see and consider it.

After a long-term marriage, you should have the self-control to give yourself a couple of months before diving into the dating world again. If your marriage has ended because of your involvement with a third-party, you will find yourself inevitably drawn to that person. But if you move too quickly after the date of separation, you'll make a mistake, add fuel to the fire, and create the impression that you were improperly engaged in a relationship before the separation. And that can become relevant to how some issues are ultimately settled.

Once you are separated, in most states, if an attempt at an amicable resolution has failed, you can then proceed with a legal action by filing a complaint in what is often called a "family or domestic court." Family courts are different from criminal and other civil courts. These are specialty courts and are sometimes limited in number and, due to this, are overworked. Some states, such as North Carolina, South Carolina, Maine, and Vermont, have several family courts, while others are just experimenting with the idea of family or domestic courts. Family courts are of limited jurisdiction, and handle only family law issues such as divorce, child custody, and domestic abuse.

In other states, family and domestic issues are heard through the regular court system and in ways that are sometimes divided by subject matter. In more rural areas, even in states that have specialized family courts, you may be assigned to the civil court docket and one of their civil court judges, should there be no local family court for that area. If there is not a family court in your district, be prepared for a long wait. The wait is typically already longer than you will like even if there is a family court, and generally longer still if you need to work through the regular court system.

Chapter 5

The Children of Divorce

Children Do Complicate the Issue

This is when we need to talk about children. If you have children and are considering divorce, read this chapter. Or if you are a friend or family member giving advice and comfort to someone with children considering a divorce, then this chapter can help put things into a better perspective.

First and foremost, children are affected by the divorce of their parents. This can't be helped, but from our experience, what can be helped is the degree and the manner that they are affected. I'll start this chapter with a personal story, one that's meant to provide a perspective on this issue. It also underlines the importance of a humane approach to divorce.

One Child's Story of Divorce:
Now I am a Divorce Attorney

I remember only a few things about my parents' divorce. We were a family. I was twelve, my sister was nine and my mother was pregnant with my other sister. It was 1966. My father was an up-and-coming doctor in Atlanta, Georgia, well respected and beloved at Emory University. My mother was a housewife, as it was known in the '60's, and we had a maid, Annie, who was a boisterous and joyous presence in our house. She baked cakes, cleaned, and allowed my mother to indulge in her own duties for the day. My mother took over the house when Annie left at 5:00 p.m. We had a family dog, Scarlet O'Hara, a silky red Irish Setter, skittish and crazy, but loved. We were incredibly lucky and a bit spoiled.

We also built a house in Sea Pines Plantation on Hilton Head Island, South Carolina in 1962, a second-row lot with a view of the ocean from a large screened-in porch. During the summer we would crab, swim, nap, swim again, build sandcastles and finally get together again for dinner. After supper, the adults would return to the porch, and we'd entertain them with sing-a-longs and skits my cousins and I performed. This would continue throughout the early evening hours, until they were sipping their cocktails as the day turned to dusk. The early evening hours, first sketched with the red of the sunset turned gray, were filled with children's voices, then dark, then bed. Even if it was still light out, my mom would close the shutters until the room was dark and lull us to sleep

We would lie in the room listening to our mothers tell their stories as their laughter grew louder penetrating the house, finally to a crescendo, usually around 10:00 pm, then dead silence. During the week, there were no men. They only seemed to appear on the weekends. When they were there, I heard my dad's stories. But this was only on weekends and maybe occasionally a week at a time when he would often be accompanied by his male friends. As time went on and I grew older, all my memories centered around my mother and my sisters, my cousins, and my friends. The summers we spent in Hilton Head, the rest of the year we were in Atlanta.

In Atlanta, I remember my dad much more vividly, in weekend touch football games with him and my friends, Atlanta Falcon

games on Sundays, and on the sideline of various football and bas-
ketball games. Until I was twelve, all I remember was a fun-loving,
handsome, God-like figure in my household that was my father.
I felt lucky. My mother was beautiful, funny, and always there for
us in her own way.

In my seventh and eighth grade years, even as a young boy, I
sensed tension in the house. The tension mounted and I began to
protect my sister from it and calm her worries. I was the only one
who would have sensed it, because I was the only one truly listening. And then it all began to fall apart. Now, as an adult, two memories stand out. The first was on a bright late Sunday afternoon
in Fall. My father and the neighborhood kids were playing touch
football when my mother, in tears, called for my father from our
porch, across the street, an object in her hand. Her look demanded
that he come to her immediately, and he did.

He left abruptly and never returned. At first, I was frozen but
kept playing, frequently glancing over at my house. In what seemed
like an instant, my father appeared on the side porch, shot me a
glance, suitcase in hand, and moved to his car. I ran feverishly to
him. When I reached him, he was crying, not angry, and he asked
me one question: "Should I go tell her goodbye?" I, at twelve years
of age, said, "No." As he drove away, I didn't wave, and I walked
inside to my mom. She was in the kitchen over the sink, eyes wet
but not crying. In her hand was picture of my father's mistress she
had found in his wallet. She was a nurse at the hospital. She turned
to me and said, "He didn't even say goodbye." I immediately took
responsibility, and she hugged me and told me empathically that
it was not my fault. Just like that, their marriage for all intents and
purposes was over

The second time vivid to my memory was around a year later. Surrounded by scandal and controversy, we moved to Hilton
Head, our summer home. My father had gone to Vietnam. It was
dusk and we were eating dinner and into our bay window stared
my father in full uniform. My mother went to the door. They

talked and I, but not my sisters, went to spend the night with him at the William Hilton Inn. There was only talk of how we were doing and what each of us was doing. The next day, he was with me and my sisters. I spent a second night with him, and then he was gone for a year.

My sophomore year, I walked across the field at my father-son night for the football team with my Uncle Sonny, not my father. There were many, many missed football games, except my senior year when he was there for almost every game. My father was stationed across the Country while in the Navy, and I played most of my rugby games without his presence, but so did the others. After all, we were adults.

There are many things that my sisters and I could use as an excuse. Divorce is not easy on children, but neither is living in a household devoid of love. You do not "stay together" for the children, sometimes you split out of compassion for them. My family felt the scars and my cousins experienced a horrific divorce, permeated by alcohol abuse, anger, and occasional violence. There is no doubt we have been affected in different ways. I can't speak for my sisters, but I can for myself. I have dealt all my life with overwhelming anxiety; psoriasis has stayed with me as a sign of it all, and I am no means perfect. In many ways I am a loner.

At the beginning of any marital breakup, you are tempted to place blame and lash out—after all, in most people's minds you've failed. And failure hurts. Almost always, you want to make excuses and assign responsibility for it all to someone else. Your spouse is an easy target. But don't attack your spouse or bitterly argue in front of, or within, earshot of your children. As for them, especially when they are young, the two of you are just mom and dad, not two people with all their flaws who were once in love. Despite everything we as children went through as a result of our parents' divorce, I can give those two great credit. I can hardly remember them ever saying a truly harsh word about each other. I didn't know who their lawyers were and never met them. I have no idea of what their financial terms were. I don't even know whether there was a court proceeding. I never talked to a judge or even a counselor.

As the years wore on, the two of them began appearing together at more and more family functions, their new spouses in tow, and not just at our own weddings, but family functions such as Christmas and Graduations. They always greeted each other affectionately.

At this point, both my mother and father have passed. I forgave them a long time ago, although there were certain times when I was growing up that I carried a lingering resentment that caused me to attack them. Thankfully, they acted as understanding adults and loved us.

The Hard-Hitting Emotional Facts of Children and Divorce

I've started this chapter so personally because I felt it was the best way to convey the message about your children. There are thousands of similar stories from children whose parents have divorced. We need to highlight the key points to grasp as we start discussing a divorce that involves children. Before we begin, from our experience, these points do need to be appreciated as hard hitting in nature. Divorce is not easy on children.

First, to children you are their parents and lifelines, not a troubled couple. You are not their friend, or just a listening ear and conduit to criticize the other spouse. You remain in their life until they or you pass away. They need you and will always need you. If you choose not to be there for them as mature and grounded adults, you should feel ashamed. As a reality check, you might read Robert Rorschach's book, *Divorce Poison*. If you try to pit your children against the other spouse, it will haunt you, and your children will pay a heavy price for such behavior.

Second, as parents you chose to bring them into the world. They do not belong in meetings with your lawyer where you are discussing your case or criticizing your spouse, period. A caring lawyer can talk to your children when they are of suitable age, which is usually around 12 and above. But they should never be dragged into the details of the proceedings.

Third, you should not ever get into physical fights or violent arguments in front of children. Young children deserve your protection, not displays of your anger and frustration, as their parents. They will figure out if there was a culprit behind the breakup of the family. They don't need to see finger-pointing or hear recriminations.

Fourth, divorce will affect the time you spend with your children, as well as the nature of your relationship. That is a fact. You might miss some of their school events, sports activities, walks in the park, and trips to the playground or pool. You will have to split shopping, BBQing, and parenting in general. Children will be affected and will feel lesser in many ways.

Fifth, the memories of today will stay with your children for their lifetimes. Divorce is always traumatic for kids, and these memories are permanent. My story in the first part of this chapter is still clear to me, and I am 70 years old now. How do you want your children to remember you as they age, and when you are no longer here on earth?

Sixth, there is fault generally to be shared by both parents. Some of you will successfully alienate your child by your own actions and some will be alienated by the actions of a vindictive spouse. The more violent and difficult the divorce is, the more the children will be damaged. That is one of the reasons for a humane approach to divorce. It's important to keep the kids out of divorce proceedings and discussions with all your power and might.

Finally, be sure to act like a parent and most of all, as a kind, civilized adult always. Sometimes friends, family members, and even your divorce attorney may try to fuel the fires of hatred. But in the long run, you will get no sympathy if you act in a way that hurts a child more than divorce normally will. This will especially influence the judges you will inevitably face. Judges have absolutely no tolerance for parents who damage children.

This chapter is to lay the groundwork for a humane divorce when children are involved. My parents acted as adults, even given how contentious their divorce may have been. It's important to try as hard as you can to leave your children less scarred by the process. Teach them to love the other parent as a parent and a person. Only on rare occasions will one parent deserve the loss of affection and love from their children.

As part of this chapter, we also need to talk about child custody, since this is often part of what fuels bad parental behaviors during a divorce proceeding.

How Does Child Custody Actually Work?

In the first part of this chapter, I've shared my personal story about being a child of divorce. Divorce does have consequences for both children and parents. This is an undisputable fact. However, the issues of divorce and children can be handled in a humane and healing manner. Unfortunately, much of the time it doesn't happen that way. Children are often manipulated as pawns to get some advantage in legal proceedings or property division decisions. Or they're used as weapons to punish and hurt the other party. Based on our experience, this is often the most volatile issue that arises in the dissolution of a marriage.

Where will your children lay their heads each night as they grow older? When will they visit the other parent? Will they play soccer at summer camps or take karate lessons? Who decides where they go to school, what instrument they can play in the band, and what car they get to drive as they get older? These are basic but serious issues, and they need to be considered carefully. There are several types of custodial agreements that should be understood.

Joint Legal Custody. Most custody agreements begin with the phrase "joint legal custody." This simply means that both parties have joint decision making about major events in the children's lives, such as medical care, education, extracurricular activities and other issues that are important to the children's lives and wellbeing. These are the important issues to all parties, both to you and your ex, as well as for the physical, mental, and emotional development of your children as people themselves who deserve the best chance at a good life.

Unfortunately, many who are going through divorce simply cannot agree on these basic issues. This happens a lot, and the courts are constantly tied up with questions regarding where the children will go to school, what activities they can participate in, and the decision-making process when one parent is not being reasonable about medical care. One thing everybody needs to understand is that in any child custody dispute the courts are going to decide in "the best interest of the minor children." What constitutes the "best interest of the minor children" is, of course, itself an important question. It's somewhat vague as a governing concept and its proper interpretation is certainly open to dispute. But this is the standard used in most courts in the country in deciding custody and other issues involving minor children.

Physical Custody. After deciding on joint legal custody, the court will then be left to decide whether the parties will have "joint physical custody." Joint physical custody essentially means an approximate 50-50 split of physical time, although the courts can decide to provide an uneven split of physical custody. In this case, one party will be designated as the primary physical custodian and the other party as the secondary physical custodian.

The difference is obvious. Pure joint custody means sharing the children on essentially an even basis. A primary and secondary physical custody designation indicates that the children are living primarily with one parent and have significant custodial time with the other. This typically could mean certain weekends or designated days. This can also involve significant time during the summer and a split of holidays. And in some cases, this would also allow for some overnight and/or afternoon visitation with the minor children that is not allotted to a weekend.

But there are certainly variations. For example, a typical weekend that goes from Friday to Sunday evening can be extended to picking up the children from school on a Thursday after school ends and returning them to school on the following Monday morning. There can also be either an overnight or dinner night with the children.

Often, a court will appoint an independent, specially trained individual to talk to the children, who then makes a recommendation to the court about child custody issues. Different states have different terms for this person. Sometimes they're called a "guardian ad litem" (GAL), and at other times they are called a "parenting coordinator" (PC) or a "child custody special master." They're usually appointed by the court when parents can't agree on custody or visitation, or there is a question about the competence of one parent. In effect, these people become the "voice of the child." In some states, GALS or PCs are non-lawyers, while in others they are generally attorneys. In some states, GALS and PCs are volunteers, while in yet others they are employed by the court system. These independent GALs or PCs will observe, talk to the parents, and talk to the children. Sometimes, parents are asked to attend parenting coordinating sessions to resolve issues. The appointed individuals then report back to the court with their recommendations.

Rarely does one parent receive no physical custody. This happens in only extreme and obvious situations, just as with documented drug use, excess bouts of drunk driving, or possible sexual or other physical abuse, where the courts feel that any unsupervised physical contact may not be in the best interest of the children, or even put them in danger.

Child custody agreements or court orders can change, however, particularly if certain circumstances change. The courts will always consider what is best for the children. If there is a change in the circumstances that affects the welfare of the minor children, the courts may revisit the custodial agreement you previously entered.

This is often called a "substantial change in circumstances," and it is generally the prerequisite and standard for changing the previous custodial agreement. What are some examples of a "substantial change in circumstances?" Here are a few.

1. ***Children Reach Age 12 or 13.*** Children reach a certain age and express an opinion as to where they want to live, and that they desire to live more with one parent or the other. This decision-making process generally happens with children when they reach the age of 12 or 13 years.
2. ***Failure of One Parent to Follow the Previous Agreement.*** Another change in circumstances can be the failure of one of the parents to adhere to the previous agreements between the parties.
3. ***Financial, Health, or Personal Difficulties.*** One parent may be experiencing certain difficulties that may make them incapable of providing for the children.

Child Custody the Humane Way

In closing on this issue of child custody, we would leave you with the following major points. First, attempt in any way you can to resolve your differences outside of a trial. You'll have plenty of opportunities to negotiate a fair solution to child custody. You can do this as a personal discussion between you and the other parent at any time in the process. If you find it difficult to carry on a good conversation face-to-face, you can always talk through your family law attorneys. Remember, your attorneys also want what's best for the children, and they can simply be your voice. Most court systems have a mandatory mediation process that allows you to decide the custodial arrangement among yourselves. In fact, court systems through the U.S. encourage you to settle or mediate the child custody issue. Sometimes the court will appoint a parenting coordinator precisely to help resolve the issues.

If you are not able to reach a solution on the custody issues, then going to court will inevitably place your personal life under a public microscope. Once this goes to court, the job of your attorney, as well as your ex-spouse's attorney, is to support their client's position. This inevitably will mean discussing under oath the most intimate details of your personal life, day-to-day behaviors, child rearing attitudes, and spending priorities. The purpose of your ex-spouse's attorney at this point is to make you look as bad as possible to the judge. This is very uncomfortable.

Always understand that the judge is going to decide these issues based on what the judge perceives is best for the children. Perception is the key word. Judges typically do not personally know you. They can only make decisions based on what's presented in court. This is what judges look at when considering child custody:

1. Your behavior both before separation and especially after the separation can weigh heavily in the judge's mind. Remember, they are deciding on custodial issues. If you are engaging in alienation of your children from the other parent or feel it's necessary to disparage or demean the other parent, especially in writing, this will not look good in a child custody hearing. It speaks to issues of character.

2. Also, be mindful that anything you put in writing can be used against you in a court of law. This includes but is not limited to the obvious texts and emails between two parties but also includes social media posts that are available to the public. This often indicates improper behaviors for a parent to be engaging in. It's absolutely amazing how many people expose their vitriol towards the other parent in texts, emails, Facebook, and other social media sites. Inevitably,

these statements are used against them once they take the stand to testify in a court of law. Simply don't engage in such immature and histrionic behavior, especially if the custody of your children is on the line.

3.   Remember to conduct yourself in a custody hearing as if you were applying for a job interview. The judge is very aware of the surroundings. If you're rolling your eyes, making audible or obvious comments, showing frustration, irritation, or disdain, or are constantly pestering your lawyer, the judge can see all these actions. If you become hostile and angry on the stand, this might also be seen as a reflection on your ability to parent your children properly, with calm and composure. In other words, during the hearing act like an adult capable of humane and proper conduct in all things.

A Note on Child Support

Child support goes hand-in-hand with child custody. We'll spend much more time on the issue of child support in a later chapter on post-divorce finances. But briefly here, in all states if the court needs to decide on child support they will use well established guidelines. For most couples with normal family incomes, the court will take your income from different sources and plug it into the formula. The formula also considers the level of custody each parent has, and possibly other issues such as medical insurance coverage.

This is all fairly straightforward, particularly if the parents are employees, with annual W-2 statements and monthly paystubs. A child support number will emerge after plugging everything into the formula, and there's very little you can do about it.

Complications in child support cases generally arise when someone is self-employed, receiving cash income, or working for 1099, sub-contractor income. Then there's often a dispute as to whether the reporting of the income is accurate. In addition, in most states the definition of what constitutes income is very broad. Again, this is discussed in more detail when we cover finances, since child support is certainly an issue of post-separation and divorce finances for everybody involved, not only for the person receiving child support, but also for the person paying the child support. The important thing is that the process of calculating child support needs to be understood by all.

Finally, always remember both child custody and child support can be agreed on by the parties without going to court. That's certainly the most preferable solution. If the parties can figure out a fair way to allocate both child custody and child support, it's great. Just be aware that, unlike property settlement agreements, the court will generally need to review both child custody and child support agreements to make sure that they are "in the best interest of the children." But unless there is something obviously or inherently wrong with these agreements, the courts will generally approve.

Chapter 6

Navigating the Divorce Legal System

It is Rarely Smooth Sailing

Let's dispel one common notion. Despite the occasional headlines you see on television programs and the inclination of Hollywood to create necessary drama to entertain the masses in dealing with issues involving the legal system, the system is not corrupt. It's true that clients often won't get what they want from the system, but that doesn't mean it's corrupt.

The domestic courts are certainly not perfect; but in my many years of practicing law, I've yet to see a crooked judge, lawyer or anybody else involved with the court system commit a crime, or "play" the system. Nearly all the people who work in the court system are honest, have integrity, and believe in the system or they'd be doing something else. There are no payoffs or political favors taking place in domestic courts.

But the legal system is a bureaucracy with a lot of rules, regulations, procedures, and deadlines. This creates both advantages and disadvantages. And it's especially true in domestic cases where parties often strongly feel that they've been grievously wronged by either their own lawyer, the lawyer on the other side, the ex-spouse, or sometimes even the judge in the final ruling of the case. That's not to say that mistakes are never made, but they are not made intentionally or maliciously, with the specific purpose of harming anyone. It's very important to know, as you enter the court process, exactly what you are facing in all facets of "the system."

The System Always Starts in the Attorney's Office

The system begins in your own lawyer's office. Paralegals, secretaries, receptionists, bookkeepers and the people who work under the lawyers in a law firm will be your most frequent contact with the legal world. If treated right, they're your biggest advocates. They're totally dedicated to your case. They are your front line, and you should cooperate with their requests to the greatest extent possible. As we've mentioned, they should not be used as a punching bag, or a target of anger. I can't count the number of times a paralegal or a secretary has been blasted by an angry client, only to have the same client talk to me in a calm and respectful manner ten minutes later when I return their call. This is always counter-productive.

Let's be clear about exactly what these people in the attorney's office typically do:

1. They take your initial phone calls, set you up in the inner-office record-keeping and document system, and give you the necessary forms to move ahead with your case. They are there for you as you move through the process.
2. They take many phone calls during a workday in addition to yours and listen as patiently and sympathetically as they can to often frustrated clients.
3. They prepare trial exhibits, put together the notebooks that harbor them, prepare an outline for the lawyer of the overall theme of the case so it can be presented in a clear and coherent manner; and deliver the final product for review by the lawyer that will constitute the presentation of your case.

4. They communicate with outside experts, such as real estate appraisers and business valuators who might work on your case.

5. On another level, many law offices will have associate lawyers who work under the lead attorney in your case. They often do legal research and prepare written legal arguments to present to the court.

6. The staff deal with the paralegals of other lawyers in exchanging the necessary information to get the case ready for trial. Sometimes they take the brunt of a disrespectful lawyer representing your ex-spouse.

7. They are computer savvy and do all the typing and preparation of the legal pleadings. Often, paralegals are so talented in preparing legal pleadings that the attorney simply tells the paralegal what they need, and that associate will put together a solid draft document. The attorney absolutely has a final say in the wording of documents, but a good paralegal is indispensable to the lawyer and to you.

8. These are the people that will be handling the calendaring of your case, the calling, scheduling the attorney's schedule and setting up appointments. They are the ones from whom you will receive most of your phone calls. They're good people. Again, it's in your best interest and the interest of the case to treat them with respect in all ways and at all times. They will certainly seek to do that with you.

The exception you might occasionally find is a staff member who either does not have the personality to persevere in the domestic law world in the first place or has simply become too burned out with the repeated issues that arise in domestic cases. Often, they simply can't handle being yelled at or disparaged by clients daily. And sometimes, that may send them over an edge where they begin to sound frustrated at the least request. I've encountered this problem on the phone with paralegals and various staff at other firms. Everybody has a bad day now and then. But few display it frequently in the world of domestic law. When they do, just remember it was probably the call before yours where somebody got on their last nerve.

Is There a Chance of Settling the Case?

Most cases do ultimately settle. This is simply part of the process. Unfortunately, in most cases, the settlement really needs to happen a lot earlier than it normally does. Remember, the process can be different between states, so make sure you talk to an attorney if you are contemplating divorce. Talk to them about your desire to settle and their preferred methods to approach settling a case. It can save a lot of time, aggravation, unpleasantness, and money. There are some broad concepts that tend to be similar across the country. Any domestic case often begins in one of two ways.

Early and Amicable Settlement Offers: The first approach to settling a case will often be an early attempt at an amicable settlement, even though on many occasions it devolves into a move toward litigation. But at least we try. In these cases, I often offer clients two options. First, I can send a fairly innocuous letter to the other party saying that I've been retained to represent their spouse in divorce proceedings and would like to hear a response from them within five days, or from their chosen attorney. On a few occasions, the recipient of the letter will simply contact their lawyer and make a good faith attempt at resolving the case on an amicable basis. What starts well and continues well should end well. This is a wise way of proceeding when possible.

If you are the recipient of such a letter, be sure that you feel comfortable with the lawyer you are talking to and sense you will be treated fairly. In most cases it's good to schedule a consultation with another lawyer to know what your rights are before you embark on attempting to proceed without representation. The initial conference is usually, at the time of this writing, anywhere from $200 to $500. These consultation fees are higher in bigger, more expensive cities, and perhaps somewhat less in many small rural areas. The consultation should give you enough information to negotiate your case on your own if you desire to do so.

Often you'll hear through the grapevine in local gossip that the lawyer your spouse has chosen "is scary" or "scares everybody." Most such lawyers, even though they may have an ominous reputation, will be more than happy to deal with you fairly in resolving your case. They are not, however, your advocate. Remember this: They work for the other party. You'll likely be better off if you have your own attorney, scary or not, at this stage.

There are new avenues in the law that you can pursue to solve your case amicably. One process is called "collaborative law," in which lawyers represent respective clients in an effort to solve the case and pledge not to appear in a trial if negotiations fall apart. That gives both sides an extra incentive to resolve any issues. In many instances, however, it's not as productive as hoped. I've also had a hard time seeing the difference between what collaborative lawyers actually do and what's done by lawyers more traditionally representing their clients.

If you are the person receiving the letter from your spouse's lawyer, you have a clear choice—either represent yourself, armed at least with some information, like what's in this book, or hire a good lawyer. The downside to this do-it-yourself approach on the part of the other spouse, if you're the one sending the letter, is that often, no response is given. Your case is then delayed for several weeks as the other party procrastinates and simply pushes it to the side as if they can wish the situation away. And this should not be surprising. Divorce is an unpleasant topic, and perhaps the other spouse doesn't agree with this solution. However, a do-it-yourself delay tactic, or any avoidance behaviors, will do nothing but prolong the inevitable and cause you considerable anxiety as you wait for your spouse's response.

We've seen amicable settlement deliberations extend for several months. This is fine as long as people are responsive and the process is taken seriously by both parties. The bottom line is that probably the most humane method for everybody involved, and the least expensive, is for both parties to give the process their full attention and work for an amicable settlement.

Forcing the Issue & Filing a Complaint. If the party contacted does not respond or at least attempt an amicable settlement of the case, a second step is inevitable: One or the other party will be "sued." That sounds scary, but it's simply the term used in the process. This usually starts with what's called a "complaint." Technically a complaint is the beginning of the process that will hopefully resolve your case in the long run.

The exact process will vary from state to state, but it typically follows certain steps. In fact, you'll have several opportunities to resolve the case without ever appearing in court, but the advantage to filing a complaint is that your spouse is almost always required to hire a lawyer and respond to the complaint within at least thirty to sixty days. In most places, the complaint involves an initial statement regarding children, child support, temporary and permanent support for a spouse, and issues regarding the division of your property.

The specific issues of support and custody will quickly be placed on the calendar for resolution and are usually done within sixty to ninety days, sometimes longer. In most places, you'll have an opportunity to resolve your custody case between the two of you in front of a mediator without your lawyers. You're strongly encouraged to do that, and if you reach a custody agreement it will be put into a proper legal form by your respective lawyers. That issue can be handled quickly if you act as responsible parents in the best interest of your children.

Post-Separation & Temporary Support

Not always, but most of the time, one of the spouses earns most of the family income. One of the chief critical issues we hear from the spouse most in need is how to survive, at least for the short-term, until things work their way through the court system. Some spouses simply have no money without a form of support. This is a devastating emotional crisis to be in. "How do I feed myself? How do I put gas in the car? What about the bills?" The problem is even more pronounced if there are minor children involved.

Certainly, the most civilized and humane thing is for the income producing spouse to continue to support, in the best way they can and within reason, the lower income earning or financially dependent spouse. This can all be worked out informally between the two spouses, and attorneys don't even need to get involved. The key idea here that we've found most useful is to seek to address this situation in the most humane way you can.

Most of the time, one spouse remains in the former marital home, often with the children, and the other spouse contributes to necessary expenses such as mortgage or rent, car payments, and utilities, as well as food and gas. In the meantime, the contributing spouse rents an apartment, sets up their own checking account, and so on. Without question, this is a humane way to financially manage the period immediately after the split. It reduces, at least to an extent, any anger, frustration, and desire to retaliate. It also sets a course for a future negotiated settlement, rather than fighting it out in the court system. However, since ultimately things will need to be decided on a more permanent basis, it's important that both spouses keep track of their expenses.

If the living and financial situation cannot be negotiated informally, and in a relatively friendly manner, the legal system in every state has a mechanism to order a form of temporary support depending on needs. This is particularly important if there are children involved. Formally, this type of support may be called by slightly different names in different states. In many states this is called "Post-Separation Support." In others, it's referred to as "Temporary Spousal Support." Whatever the name, it has the same purpose: to provide a period of temporary financial support until things can be decided on a more permanent basis.

Temporary spousal support, however, is a legal and court ordered process. It only happens if a formal complaint is filed with the court as discussed above. An attorney will need to start this process, and generally there is a request for temporary spousal support when the legal divorce complaint is filed. A court ordered spousal support creates a legal obligation of one spouse to pay the other, at least until arrangements are made on a more permanent basis. Spousal support is usually provided in the form of monthly payments to the dependent spouse.

The court will decide on temporary spousal support based on a variety of factors, such as the expenses of the separating spouses, the age and health of the parties, their living arrangements, the debts and assets of the spouses, the earning capacities of the spouses and their ability to cover costs, whether children and child custody decisions are involved, the length of the marriage, and other things.

When going into a temporary spousal support hearing, make sure you have put together all your expense records in detail, including utility payments, food costs, gas receipts, mortgage or rent obligations, credit card expenses, clothes shopping, car payments and insurance—in short, everything. Go back in time, particularly since some expenses are yearly, such as real estate taxes. You need to be able to prove what you are claiming for household expenses. You also need to prove income, with recent paystubs, or if you own a business, a recent internal financial statement showing income. Your attorney will provide you with what is often known as an "Expense Affidavit," which will list detailed categories of monthly expenses to assist you in the process. Often, these expense affidavits must be filed with the court within a set time.

Note that some courts consider "earnings capacity," which means that the court might decide you could get a job in the future, even if you're not presently working. This is particularly common if you worked previously and have a clear profession that you could go back into, such as being a nurse, dentist, or teacher.

The purpose of temporary spousal support is to make sure that both spouses can meet their financial needs until things are decided on a more permanent basis. That will usually be the date when the courts make the final decision, although the parties can agree to a different specific date, if they want, when the temporary spousal support will end. Although it's meant to be a stopgap until the final support decisions are made, the courts can alter the temporary support order if the situation changes dramatically, such as that the higher earning spouse is fired, or one spouse develops a disabling illness or injury. In some states, temporary support may go beyond simple household maintenance and include a type of temporary alimony.

Courts are also directed to consider the "accustomed style of living." Frankly, from my experience, that's seldom an issue. It's always more expensive to support two households than one. That's a simple fact. In addition, there are new expenses, including attorney fees.

Any type of temporary support, as well as temporary child custody and child support, are generally put in place until there is a final resolution, either through settlement or mediation or (try to avoid this) a ruling by a court after a hearing. Note, however, that any final support decisions by the court do not have to follow the payment schedule made for temporary support.

Attorneys, the court system, and certainly most parents will put minor children at the top of their list of priorities. Once you have resolved the issue of child custody, child support is usually easy to determine, since it is almost always based on a formula, regardless of which state you are in. The calculation of child support is covered in detail in a later chapter.

If child support and any initial spousal support is resolved by the parties in mediation or by mutual agreement, these will be one of the first issues that will appear on the calendar. Rarely is this decided immediately, despite the desires of the spouse most at financial risk. The process can take anywhere from thirty to ninety days before a temporary spousal support case is heard. But remember, these early support issues, such as child support and spousal support, are only designed to be temporary, to get people through to the final decision that's generally made in court on a later date, or resolved by the parties and put into an approved permanent contract.

Once child custody, and other initial and temporary support issues are resolved, you might be in for a long wait. The division of property remains to be addressed, as well as final decisions on spousal support or alimony. Temporary child custody and child support decisions can also be challenged, negotiated, or decided by a final court decision.

Getting Ready for the Case

Now it all becomes pretty legalistic. The next steps involve getting the information necessary to either resolve your case or have a judge decide it in a court proceeding. There are several parts of this process.

Getting the Information - Discovery. Once a complaint is filed, the next step is inevitably "discovery." Different states might use slightly different terms, but the terminology below is probably the most common. The discovery process involves information and documents that will be exchanged between the lawyers. These are usually in the form of questions called "Interrogatories," which are questions about your case and estate. There is also a request for various documents that are necessary for the case, known as a

"Request for Production of Documents." This generally requires you to hand over bank statements, credit card statements, and other financial documents. If a business is involved, the request will probably also be for various business documents, including tax returns, internal financial statements, general ledgers, and various other related documents. These requests are usually detailed and involve probably more than what's really needed. But attorneys tend to ask for everything for a reason. First, they may not get another chance, and second, it gives both parties a sense of the time it will take to gather up all relevant documents, as well as hinting at the time they may need.

On occasion, a document called a "Request for Admissions" is directed at you, in which you are asked specific questions that you must answer, on a yes or no basis.

Many times, clients simply adopt the attitude that they have no desire to answer the questions posed to them. The fact is that most questions that are asked will simply have to be answered. Your attorney might want to object to some questions if they think they aren't relevant, but the best strategy at the front end is to just answer them all. If you are the person who has received the interrogatories and request for documents from your ex-spouse, rather than arguing with the paralegals who are attempting to answer the questions sufficiently for the other side, it's far more productive for you to spend some time on the questions and let your lawyer decide which answers should be provided and which should not. That's our job and not yours. Your task is to answer in an honest and forthright manner all the questions asked.

Getting to Interview People – The Deposition. After discovery is completed there may be a need, in certain cases, for a process called "depositions." Depositions are simply mechanisms for the lawyer on the other side of your case to learn more about your position in the case, and vice versa. Personally, I'm a firm believer in simply gathering information from the other client in a friendly and non-combative manner and atmosphere. That approach often leads to getting more information. Formal depositions might be necessary, though, in more complex cases, as for example in those involving the ownership of a business.

Depositions are scheduled. Most likely you will be formally notified by a "Notice of Deposition," although sometimes it's done more informally with your attorney. Depositions almost always take place in one of the lawyer's offices. There will be a court reporter recording the proceedings. You will be sworn in. The deposition gives the attorney who called for it the right to ask questions. You need to answer those questions. Your attorney will be present for the deposition, and possibly object to some of the lines of questioning. You don't need to be nervous about it but simply tell the truth. If you're going in for a deposition, you'll almost always have a conference with your attorney beforehand. Typically, depositions last between 2 and 4 hours, depending on the complexity of the case. Some are longer, and others shorter. Also, almost always the opposing attorney will ask that you bring documents with you. Make sure you do. In the post-Covid world, some depositions now still take place online using Zoom or some other web-based conference system. It's easier for all involved.

The use of depositions needs to be considered strategically. They are necessary at times. First, many of the questions asked by your attorney at a deposition have been posed by you, as the client. Almost always, your attorney will confer with you prior to the deposition. Second, the attorney will also need to speak with your experts, such as business valuators, real estate appraisers, and accountants, if the case involves these types of issues, to make sure the questions your experts have are also answered. The other side will probably do the same.

Depositions certainly provide information and an opportunity to get questions answered. In fact, in many states, they are formally called "Discovery Depositions," with guidelines as to what can be asked. Other states give more leeway to the questions properly asked.

Surprisingly, many attorneys don't really understand the strategic nature of depositions. The authors of this book, one from the attorney perspective who has taken hundreds of depositions in his career, and one from the expert witness side, who has been deposed close to a hundred times, both think it's a terrible strategic error when lawyers use depositions to cross examine the person being deposed, almost like they're trying the case in court. Some states, such as California, have strict parameters for depositions, specifying that it's simply to gather information rather than for any sort of psychological intimidation or gamesmanship.

But from our experience, attorneys make this mistake a lot. Asking what are more properly cross-examination questions in a deposition is counterproductive since it prepares the other side for what's coming at the trial. These short-sighted attorneys often play all their cards prior to the trial. This informs everybody of exactly where they will be coming from in the case, and so allows the other side time to rebut their arguments when the case actually goes to trial. Quite frankly, depositions in our opinion should be purely about discovery, and not a time to argue the case.

Another strategic part of the deposition is also important. The deposition provides an opportunity for the attorneys to see how the opposing spouse, experts, and other people that are being deposed will act and respond during a trial if they're called to testify. It is almost like a trial interview. If you sound professional, not nervous, but confident, well prepared and honest in a deposition, the other attorney probably might think twice about going to court, and instead recommend to their client a settlement. These are just some ideas to keep in mind.

Another aspect that's totally inexcusable in depositions is un-professionalism and rudeness. A partner of mine recently attended a deposition in which the lawyer abused the "f-word" in front of several women on more than one occasion. This is inexcusable for any lawyer. It should not be tolerated by you or your attorney. A good advocate will vigorously object to any form of unprofessionalism by the other lawyer. And start questioning your representation if it's your attorney acting unprofessional. Lawyers want their questions answered correctly, efficiently and honestly, but that's really all the deposition should be. It's not a battlefield.

A Time to Pause: The Mediation

After the depositions and interrogatories have taken place, you will then be required in most jurisdictions to go to what is known as a "mandatory mediation." Most mediations are non-confrontational, in the sense that you and your lawyer will not be in the same room as your ex-spouse and his or her attorney.

Some mediations can begin with face-to-face contact. There may be some jurisdictions that still do this, but I would highly recommend that you ask your lawyer to conduct the mediation in a different way. I find that bringing everybody together with a mediator, except for a statement about conducting the mediation, results too often only in counter-productive hostility and early accusations. My strong suggestion to mediators, clients, and lawyers is that you stay in different rooms as the mediator explains the process to both parties and attempts to resolve your case.

Mediators must take courses in mediation. In the domestic field, most mediators are also highly experienced domestic lawyers. Some mediators are apparently taught simply to convey offers back and forth between the two rooms. I personally find this to be nonproductive. I strongly invite the mediator's active involvement, especially one who is a good and experienced lawyer. Making subtle and insightful suggestions as to whether you are being unreasonable and where the law will take you if you continue a course of action is helpful and leads to settlement. You might ask your attorney for this type of active mediator, rather than one with a more passive approach. You will have to pay the mediator for their time, as well as your attorney's time.

Also note that an actual agreement might not come out of mediation, but often in the following weeks the parties will get into more of a settlement mode. Hopefully, you can settle the case before a trial. Many times, the settlement comes literally in the court room, prior to the trial—a deal on the proverbial "courthouse steps." Take our advice to heart: if you want to settle, let the mediation work. That's the best solution, and it's why many states require mediation. In any event, try to settle the case much earlier than waiting until the trial date. That's really the best and most humane way of dealing with all of this. Settlements, whether in mediation or with attorneys talking by phone, require the will of both parties. One side being unreasonable will always prolong the process. Waiting to the trial date also becomes much more expensive, since your attorneys, their office staff, and your experts, if any, will have spent a lot of time getting ready for the trial. You are financially responsible for their time.

The Dreaded (and Expensive) Trial

This is really the last step. Data on this are slim, but one recent study found that over 90% of domestic cases settle prior to trial, with fewer than 10% moving to the trial phase. From our experience, that's on target. A trial will take a considerable amount of time, and most judges' calendars are extremely crowded. This will almost always mean a long wait for your case to be heard. Trials also carry a heavy bill. Preparing and conducting a trial hearing is probably the most expensive part of a divorce case.

Preparing for Court: Preparation for a trial means that your lawyer does a considerable amount of work in advance to present your case in the best possible way. Domestic case trials are almost always held before a judge. They are not jury trials. A one-or two-day trial is not an enjoyable experience for anyone except the lawyers. Complicated cases, involving businesses, a lot of real estate, and investments will take much longer.

A trial means you're handing your entire life, in a condensed form, to a stranger, the judge who knows nothing about you. Judges are usually smart and honorable people who will be doing the best they can despite having an onslaught of facts thrown at them in a short period of time. This is not the most effective way to resolve a domestic case and never will be. But if things can't be settled in advance, it's the only remaining solution. Some people think they want "their day in court." But it's rarely a good experience with the desired results.

Don't let yourself think that the court system is going to be the answer to all your problems. Also, don't indulge in fancifully assuming you'll win your case simply because you feel you're the righteous party, or the victim in the proceedings, or that your spouse is the perpetrator of ill will and hardship inflicted on your family. Trial judges need to consider all the evidence and follow the law. It's not a movie whose outcome you can write and direct. As obvious as this is, you'd be surprised how common this fantasy attitude is with clients. Always remember, that the judge will hear two sides to every story.

The timing of the entire process depends on what state and even county you are in. No matter what, though, it's not fast. Some states seem to work at it faster than others. We found that Texas is one of the fastest states to get a domestic case heard in trial. The typical time, however, can be 12 to 18 months before both attorneys are ready to go and there is an available trial date for all parties. An additional frustration is that if the case doesn't finish up in the assigned time, it might be months before the judge can schedule another time to wrap it up.

In larger communities with a lot of divorces, even though you're assigned a judge, all the judges have tremendous caseloads, and your case will slowly meander through the process until it ages enough that the court must hear it. Terms of court usually last from one to two weeks and the fact that your case appears on a "court calendar" that comes out the week before the established court date does not necessarily mean that your case will be reached then and heard. It all depends on how many cases are before you. You also do not need to appear on the first day of any court proceedings unless you're informed to do so by your lawyer. You'll be told specifically what time and place your case will be heard, and any good lawyer will bring you in for preparation before the case goes to trial.

You will probably be called to testify. At other times, you will likely be sitting next to your attorney as other people testify— some on your behalf and some for your ex. Talk to your attorney about proper trial behavior. Here are our recommendations in a nutshell:

1. Your attorney will most certainly "prep" you for testifying. Listen well to what they recommend.
2. It's natural to be nervous on the stand. Just take a deep breath and try to relax.
3. Dress nicely. Ask your attorney how you should dress when testifying.
4. Always be honest and truthful.
5. Answer only the question asked. You can give an explanation but stay on point.
6. Don't ramble. You don't have to give voice to every thought you have.
7. Always act professionally, and occasionally look at the judge.
8. Never lose your temper. Understand that part of the strategy of the opposing attorney is to make you look bad, and nothing looks worse than losing your temper.
9. If you need to take a break for the restroom, tell the judge. They understand.

10. You don't need to look at your spouse. Ignore whatever faces they're making.
11. If your attorney objects to something, immediately stop talking, even in mid-sentence. The judge will say whether the objection is overruled, and you can talk again, or the judge might sustain the objection, and the attorney needs to ask the question in a different way. You need to be quiet when the judge and the attorneys are discussing the objections.

We have four recommendations when other people are testifying.

1. You will probably be sitting next to your attorney when other people are testifying. Dress nicely all the time, even if you're not testifying.
2. As you sit next to your attorney, you can write comments or questions on a piece of paper to communicate back and forth. Talk to your attorney ahead of time about this.
3. Make sure you do not make faces, sneer, shake your head, sigh loudly, or make choking sounds when your ex-spouse or their experts are testifying. Remember, the judge can see and hear everything, and this does not come across well.
4. Talk things over at breaks and lunches. You might be able to give some insights to your attorney for the next round of questions.

Waiting for the Decision

After the Trial: Now comes the wait. After the trial, in most cases, except for custody cases, you will be waiting a fair amount of time for a final decision in your matter. Judges are presented with a tremendous amount of information during a trial and will need to go back and absorb that information before they make a final ruling. Sometimes they get it wrong, and sometimes they get it right, depending on your perspective. Sometimes you're shocked by their decision and extremely disappointed, sometimes you're happy with it. But if you don't like the result, try to remember that you could have settled earlier. Ultimately, you've left the decision to the judge. People who simply let the court decide often seriously regret that decision in the end, but it's too late by then. There are times when one client is very happy with the decision. It's usually the more reasonable client who emerges basically intact. Regardless, always remember that you're handing your life over to a judge who has a limited amount of time to learn about you and the facts and circumstances that led to the dissolution of your marriage. If children are involved, those from the age of twelve or above can normally speak privately with judges in chambers. But even this can't guarantee you the result you most want.

If there are significant investments, real estate, property, and businesses involved, the judge has even more difficult decisions to make. Remember, judges don't typically have advanced degrees and work experience in economics or business, and so they can often get things wrong, but it is not out of malice. Quite frankly, some court decisions can seem like a toss of a coin. This is another reason to just settle.

The Appeals Process: Finally, if either party does not like the results of their court proceedings, there is the option of appeals, which are taken up to a higher court. Many people have a misunderstanding about what the higher courts do in reviewing appealed cases. There are several common misconceptions about the appeals process.

First and foremost, the Appellate Court is reviewing only the record placed before it and it makes its decision based on that record as to whether an error was made by the judge. A transcriber will present a transcription of the entire trial to the Appellate Court. Each party will be allowed to submit appellate briefs or memoranda that indicate what each lawyer feels the facts are and what the law should be. In most cases, appellate decisions are made by reading the record and hearing the arguments through the form of written briefs in the Appellate Court.

Second, there are various standards that are very strict that can allow an Appellate Court to overturn a trial judge's opinion. The fact of the matter is that most trial judge opinions are confirmed on appeal. Your lawyer will not be able to present additional evidence before the Appellate Court and you will not be able to testify again before the Appellate Court or present additional witnesses. You're simply stuck with the record that was built up during the trial level and a review of that record. Sometimes appellate decisions come down that make history or "precedent" for cases that will be heard in the future and that allow lawyers a database from which to retrieve cases that are like the situation they're currently facing.

Third, the Appellate Courts are not required to adopt either party's argument, and they often issue opinions that seem to be a hybrid of arguments that were made at the lower court by the respective lawyers. A different result is not guaranteed or even likely. You and your case are at the whim of an appellate judge's opinion about how the trial was conducted and whether the law was followed. The Appellate Court can also send the case back for another trial. And it just gets more and more expensive for you.

Fourth, and obviously, it takes even longer to get to a resolution if you appeal. After waiting for what seems like forever to get to trial in your domestic case, you will wait just as long, if not longer, to hear an opinion from the Appellate Court. This wait can last up to a year and a half. As an example, suppose your case began through the system 18 months ago and was finally heard before the court in, let's say, October of this year. There may be several weeks, if not months, before the judge makes a final decision, which may arrive right after the first of the new year. If you appeal, it will take approximately 100 to 120 days to present what is known as a "record on appeal," which consists primarily of the transcript of the hearings that were held before the trial court. We're now maybe four more months into the new year.

On very few occasions, lawyers are invited to make oral arguments before Appellate Courts. Most Appellate Courts have dispensed with that formality. If lawyers are invited to the Appellate Court to make what's known as an "oral argument," or an argument in person, that may mean that there is some special significance that the Appellate Court is giving your case. After oral arguments, which, again, are rare in domestic cases, you are then subjected to another considerable stretch of time waiting for the Appellate Court decision. While this is a great financial boon for lawyers, it's an absolute major drain on your income, and adds the stress and frustration of waiting even longer for a final decision on your case. This is also taxing on ex-spouses who want to get on with their lives. Cases can be slow, whether in populated urban areas or small counties. The above scenario is typical. In some jurisdictions, cases might get heard much more quickly, but in others, cases will take longer. Either way, it's a long process.

Even in states with a family court system, many rural counties still don't have a family court. In these circumstances, the regular court system will be assigned to handle any type of domestic matter. These counties have also begun to adopt mediation to keep people out of court. In these locations, however, it could take you much longer to get on the court calendar simply because the time in these systems is extremely limited, and court dates do not occur as frequently as in larger counties. Either way, the process will probably frustrate you. Add on appeals and it's much worse. We point this out so that you will seriously consider doing whatever it takes to avoid the lengthy and uncertain process of trial, or trial and appeal. You will want to get on with your life.

The Nice People Who Work at the Courthouse

Litigation is a complex process. It's useful to know a little bit about the "characters of the courthouse." This is important, since your attorney and their staff might be throwing terms around you need to understand. It's their everyday language but is not likely yours. And they can easily forget this as they speak to you, and to each other in your presence.

Court Clerks: These people are dedicated public servants and are willing to do virtually anything for you. They are underpaid, but very smart, talented, and hard workers. They manage a massive court system along with the Judge who is appointed to your case. They keep all cases going in an organized and efficient manner. What they do is extremely important. Clerks move the process forward in the court system. In any case you try, there will be a clerk in your courtroom. They're there to record the process as your case is being tried, and to follow any instructions the judge gives them, as well as to listen to your case. You'll have virtually no direct personal contact with court clerks. They are mysterious people who appear and disappear in and out of the courtroom at different times and places. They are, however, integral to the process. We are all glad for what they do.

Bailiffs: These individuals are often county Sheriff's Department members that have been stationed around the courthouse to protect the individuals who are trying your case from any danger or violence. In some states, they are court officers hired specifically to protect the courtroom. In some locales, these folks are called constables or marshals, or they might be part of another local law enforcement agency. On rare occasion, as you've likely seen on TV, these brave men and women will dive into action to protect the people they are there to serve. Watch your lawyer as he or she walks into the courtroom. See what type of relationship they have with the clerks and the bailiffs. If there are smiles or friendly banter, and they seem glad to see your lawyer, then rest assured that you are probably in good hands.

Trial Court Administrators: Not every jurisdiction in the country has these administrators, but generally each judge in such a place has what is known as a trial court administrator. They handle a tremendous case load and do everything in their power to get your case put on the judge's court calendar. Just remember that people at the courthouse talk among themselves. Judges feel very protective of these associates. If somebody demeans a courthouse worker, or acts rudely over the phone to them, it will likely trickle down to your judge and could affect your case.

Quick Comment on Judges: The final thing I will say about "The System" is about the judges themselves. You need to know one basic thing: These are good people. They are legally trained in the system. But just like any group, they all have different personalities. My experience with judges over forty years has been largely positive. Of course, we should all remember that judges are also human. On a particular day, they may carry their own emotions into the courtroom, although they struggle not to do so. In fact, it may happen more often than you might think. They are professionals who have a very difficult job. They are certainly fallible and have their proclivities towards certain aspects of domestic law. And judges may not completely understand the complexities of some things they hear, such as when your expert economists or accountants talk about complex investments, bookkeeping, financial reporting, and business valuation issues. As in any profession, some are more comfortable with such complex issues than others. Your lawyer should have experience in dealing with the judges in your jurisdiction and know what their proclivities are and should be able to be honest with you about what you may face when you go into their courtroom.

If you go this far and are willing to try your case, it's extremely important that you realize you are going into what's very much like a big job interview and that your behavior will likely have a tremendous impact on the outcome of your case. After all, the case is about you and not just the other party. In fact, treat your testimony as you would a job interview for a position you really want. Your approach should be one in which you are trying to convince the judge that you are someone who can be believed and that you are a good person. That is often more difficult in the microcosm of a courtroom than you might think. A person's life and character, in the focused course of a trial, is reduced to a very incomplete story played out as best it can be in a relatively short period of time. Therefore, any impression you make in this context is extremely important, because it will matter. When you come across as a wise, good, and humane individual, things are likely to go much better.

Some Final Comments About the System

In the end, solving cases quickly is up to the primary participants, the two main parties involved, and depends on them even more than the attorneys and judges. There are many opportunities along the way, some of them informal like talking with your spouse, or communicating through your attorneys, and some are more formal, like mediation, to resolve any primary differences without going to court. Court should really be considered a last resort in domestic cases. We hope we have communicated this well. It's often hard for people to believe, but a court trial is best avoided. This means you'll need to be flexible, and likely far more flexible than is comfortable or easy for you, in order not to end up in court. But if you do end up in a trial, you need an attorney who can perform well in court.

One thing that neither you, nor your lawyer, can control is the court calendar. In larger communities and cities, the court calendar can become extremely crowded, and judges will pick and choose the case they want to hear at a particular time. In smaller counties there may be fewer courts and limited time to hear your case. The bottom line is the system will frustrate you; but your lawyer will try as hard as possible to get your case on the calendar and heard.

Too often, I see the clients coming back into the system, especially in custody disputes. Some people linger in the system for years with motions and counter motions, motions for contempt, and constant battling. In a perverse way, it seems they almost enjoy it. But there are many other enjoyments far less expensive and better for anyone to experience.

Over the years, I've adopted a personal rule: If I agree to represent you, then I'll represent you for the first time. There are some people I really like and who, in turn, also seem to like me a lot. For these folks, I can represent them a second time. But more often, since the process is so exhausting, people get burned out on the lawyer who represented them the first time around, or the old lawyer is worn out with you. In this instance, it may be wise to seek other representation. In most domestic cases, no matter how good the client is and how good the lawyer is, the client may have some misgivings about the experience that they had with their first lawyer. That is simply the nature of the beast. A fresh start may help.

Chapter 7

TYPES OF PROPERTY

Value and Division

Finances are a big part of the divorce process. Finances are also one of the most confusing. We have two chapters that specifically address the issues of divorce finances. This chapter is on the division of assets or property during a divorce process. The division of property needs to be understood by all parties. What needs to be understood is not only the process by which assets are divided, but how they are typically valued. The next chapter addresses an issue that is extremely stressful—financial survival after divorce. The information provided below is based in working on the financial aspects with hundreds, if not thousands of couples going through divorce where significant property and assets were involved. This discussion is meant to be neither formal financial advice nor legal advice, but rather simply to provide the most important insights that can be discussed with your attorney. Remember, rules are subject to regular change through the passage of new laws and legislation, decisions in appellate and higher courts, ballot initiatives, and even the interpretation by different judges in the gray areas.

A Word About Equitable Distribution v. Community Property

Nine states in the country have "community property" laws, while the remaining states are called "equitable distribution" states. As of the writing of this book, the nine community property states are Arizona, California, Idaho, Louisiana, Nevada, New Mexico, Texas, Washington, and Wisconsin—primarily western states. In these community property states, spouses own and owe everything equally; however, for this to apply, an asset or property, or debt, needs to be considered marital. Generally, with a couple of exceptions, anything acquired during the marriage in a community property state is considered marital. In most community property states, marital property is divided 50-50 between the spouses. However, in these community property states, inheritances and gifts to one party are not generally considered marital, nor are any assets acquired before marriage.

This actually sounds exactly like most equitable distribution (ED) states. The major difference is not so much how an asset is classified as being marital or not, but rather how the marital component is divided. Whereas many community property states almost require a 50-50 split of marital assets, equitable distribution states try to be perhaps a little fairer, and so we get the term "equitable distribution." But in being fair, it's also more complicated. Only marital assets are subject to equitable distribution decisions.

The major difference in ED states is that the judge has much more leeway in the division of assets in the effort to arrive at what's "equitable." Most ED states, through their state statutes, provide guidelines for the judge to follow in an equitable distribution of assets and debts.

In general, the starting point in an ED state assumes a 50% split of marital assets like a community property state, but then the judge can consider things like: length of the marriage, individual income, and the future earning potential of each spouse, the age and health of the spouses, contributions to the marriage both financial and non-financial, the future financial needs and prospects of each spouse, custodial responsibilities for children, who should own or occupy the marital residence, any deferred compensation one spouse might get, any contributions of a spouse to the education or career of the other spouse, and contributions of a spouse to increase the value of separate property. Regardless of whether your state is a community property state or an equitable distribution state, they all share the same type of assets and valuation issues with a few exceptions.

What is "Property"

Before we dive deeper, remember that property is defined very broadly. Essentially, property is defined as something that somebody can have a title to or own. Of course, things like real estate, cars, furniture, investments in the stock market, and pensions are all property. Businesses are also considered property, since they often own assets themselves, have the ability to generate income, and are owned by a spouse. These types of property or assets are what 95% of divorce cases deal with. But property can also mean things like copyrights, music rights, patents, trade secrets, and other highly complicated issues related to "intellectual property," often known to hipsters, creatives, and tech moguls as "IP." Even ideas, if they are valuable, developed enough through research and effort, and could lead to a future patent or benefit, can be considered "property." For example, a cure for the common cold would be very valuable, even if not fully developed to the patent stage. If you have any important property issues, such as intellectual property, then make sure to talk about it with your attorney as early as possible.

Let's look at some of the key issues related to property matters.

The Important Dates of Divorce and Property

There are generally three key dates to identify property and their values. The date of marriage, the date of separation/cut-off date (depending on your state) for valuation, and the date of settlement through mediation or agreement, or by a trial with a judge's verdict. Attorneys often like to use abbreviations for these dates, such as DoM, DoS, DoV and DoT.

In some states, the date of physical separation is the important cut-off date, while in other states it might be the date of filing the petition for divorce. The date used is important for the purpose of identifying property, whether the property is marital or separate property, and for determining their values. This important date is determined by the rules of a particular state.

In all cases, property, regardless of its nature, such as cars, furniture, investments, real estate, businesses, and all other assets, as well as anything owed on these assets, will need to be classified and valued as of the key cut-off or trigger dates in your state regarding marital property. The other dates become important if there are assets or property acquired prior to the marriage, or if there is an argument for unequal distribution in equitable distribution states, or there is a significant increase or decrease in value up to the actual date of division. Don't worry. You won't have to figure all this out on your own. You can rely on suitable experts, or on your lawyer, with additional expert guidance.

As previously mentioned, different states have different definitions for this very important trigger date to define marital property. In this book we talk primarily about the date of separation, since even states that might have a different cut-off date for defining separate or marital property, or if a property increases or decreases in value from the date of separation to the date of trial, judges will often consider this in their final decision—particularly in equitable distribution states.

When it comes to the topic of property, these are very important issues that you'll need to discuss with your attorney—the cut-off date for defining marital property and the key dates for having your property and assets valued. There are many cases, for example, where one spouse received a significant amount of money after physical separation, but the courts still viewed these funds as marital property since in that state there were different cut-off dates.

Note that in states that use a date of separation as the key valuation date, you may need to prove that you were physically separated with evidence such as sworn statements from friends and family, separate utility bills or leases, bank accounts with different addresses, and so on. In states that use filing for the date of legal separation or a petition for divorce as the key date, the date is simple to determine.

The date of division, by trial or settlement agreement, often becomes important since property values can sometimes change dramatically between the date of separation/cut-off and the date of settlement or trial. Think of what happened during the Covid-19 period. If you owned a small restaurant and got separated right before Covid-19, the restaurant might have been doing quite well and could have significant value as of the date of separation. But then Covid-19 hit, everything got closed by government edicts, and your restaurant might have been forced to go out of business. If your divorce trial was right after Covid-19, your business may have no value as of the date of trial or settlement. Likewise, residential real estate properties jumped in value during much the same time. The judge, particularly in an ED state, can consider all this.

Note that the above discussion about cut-off dates when assets become separate versus marital, and when assets are valued, are determined by state laws. Most property issues in divorce are settled without going to court. It's far better to have the parties agree on a valuation cut-off date for property. It's easier for the experts and the attorneys. For purposes of settlement, we strongly recommend the date of physical separation as the key date for property valuation. This is really when the marriage relationship ends, emotionally and physically. But if you agree to a particular date, this needs to be a binding agreement by all. And if the case cannot settle, you still will need to get a date of trial value in addition to the date of separation value.

Almost always, your attorney and your ex-spouse's attorney, will put together a computerized spreadsheet that identifies all the different assets/properties involved in the marriage, as well as all the different financial obligations and debts in the marriage as of the dates described above. They will then identify these assets and liabilities as being either marital or separate. The attorneys will finally put a value on the different assets as of the different dates. On completion, the spreadsheet will also identify which assets and liabilities each of the parties want to retain after the divorce.

These spreadsheets are key. They are how we figure out what's owed to whom. If one party is keeping more assets than the other, then that person will need to give some other assets or pay to the other spouse to balance it out. This is all calculated on the spreadsheets. When it comes to property, the spreadsheets are what summarize everything.

However, be aware that there will likely be very different opinions about the assets, when they were acquired, whether they are marital or separate, how much they are worth, and who gets to keep them. It's often fascinating to see how the spreadsheets can differ so much between the parties, particularly at the beginning of the process. But realize that this is all part of the negotiations and property settlement discussions.

Differences in the spreadsheet values point to the issues that need to be discussed in more detail, or if ultimately an outside expert needs to get involved to help determine the value. If the spreadsheet shows similar values on an asset, the parties can agree or "stipulate" to that value, and that's the end of it, at least for that piece of property.

If the case is not settled, the judge will ultimately decide. But remember that when it comes to property, assets, and liabilities, it's all put down in a computerized spreadsheet. Even the judge will work from a spreadsheet listing all the assets, properties, and obligations at trial.

Marital v. Separate Property

A first look at the assets or property involved in a marriage is always whether they are considered separate property versus marital property.

Property Owned Prior to Marriage: In most states, the first type of separate property consists of assets a person had prior to the marriage and were subsequently brought into the marriage. These can be stocks, bonds, pensions, furniture, jewelry, and real estate that were acquired by one spouse prior to the marriage. Businesses, the topic of another chapter, can also be considered separate when brought into marriage. Both parties in a marriage may have such separate assets.

Since divorce is covered by state laws, each state is a little different. There are a few states, such as Indiana, Connecticut, and South Dakota, where property acquired prior to the marriage, even a pension, becomes "marital" property upon the marriage. These states are called "All Property" or "one-pot" states. Not surprisingly, one tends to see prenuptial agreements more often in "All Property" or "one-pot" states. States that are "All Property" tend to give the judge much greater latitude in making distribution decisions, particularly for short marriages. In most states, however, property acquired prior to the marriage is considered separate property unless there is action taken during the marriage to make it "marital."

In some states, there is special consideration given to the marital home. In these states, if one partner brought a residence into the marriage and it became the primary "marital" home, it is considered now marital even if it remains titled in the original owner's name. Some states put greater emphasis on the notion of "use" during the marriage, rather than ownership. For example, in these states, a car brought into the marriage, if "used" extensively by both spouses, is now considered marital, while other property, such as a stock portfolio, acquired prior to the marriage might still be considered separate.

A good website that shows how each state defines marital versus separate property, and what the key cut-off dates are for defining marital versus separate property is the one at www.divorcenet. com/states/nationwide/property_division_by_state.

Property Acquired During Marriage: The other types of assets that can be considered separate are gifts and inheritances, usually from other family members, that are made specifically to a spouse as distinct from the couple, even though they are in a marriage.

However, an asset that is purchased during the marriage is generally assumed to be marital. This is almost always the case. Think of it this way: if the asset is purchased during the marriage, it is a marital asset unless one party can show it is not marital. Proving an asset purchased during the marriage is not marital is both difficult and complicated. It generally involves showing that the asset was intentionally and specifically acquired with a person's separate property and that there was clear action taken during the marriage to keep it separate. This is often called the "source of funds" argument. Suppose a person getting married had a $100,000 CD prior to the marriage. After the marriage, the CD matured, and the person simply bought another CD with that money in their individual name. It's probably still separate property, even though this last CD was acquired during the marriage. However, suppose after cashing in the CD, the spouse contributed to buying a marital home and puts the marriage partner on the deed. This is something that has now become much more complicated and needs to be explored with an attorney. In many states there is another concept, that of "gifting" separate property to the "marital estate." That means one spouse in a marriage can specifically and intentionally (and sometimes unintentionally) transfer their separate property to the marriage, and then it becomes a marital asset.

What then constitutes a gift to the marital estate? Every state has different rules and case law around this, and much of this is determined by showing intent. In many states, the simple fact of "co-mingling" assets during the marriage points to intent. This is a complication that needs to be discussed carefully with an attorney to see how to deal with it.

Property Acquired After Separation: Suppose you and your spouse decide to physically separate, get your own residence and bank accounts, pay your own bills, and start buying your own property such as furniture or cars, as well as acquiring debt on some of these purchases. Two years later, your spouse decides to formally file for divorce. This is a typical scenario in many marital break-ups. In some states, the property and debt you both accrue after the date of separation would be considered separate, while in other states, it might still be considered marital. And of course, this is confusing.

We have discussed the importance of understanding the cut-off date in your state regarding whether something is considered marital or separate. In some states, the cut-off date is the date of physical separation. In most other states, the cut-off date is a particular legal action, such as filing for divorce or a legal separation. In yet other states, there is more discretion given to judges after they hear testimony.

Final Comments About Separate v. Marital Property: Not surprisingly the marital versus separate property issue is one of the biggest areas of conflict, since only marital property is usually divided. This can be quite detailed and complicated. This is an issue that can also get quite nasty, since how property is divided will often define the financial future of the parties involved. If there are a lot of assets at stake, it often ends up in court where the judge needs to make the decision. Hopefully, the parties can settle this issue before it gets to court. You at least get to use your own judgment and have a measure of control during settlement. But that all ends at trial, which is again part of why we continue to recommend settling and not going to trial.

For obvious reasons, longer marriages tend to have more marital property while shorter marriages might have more separate property. Second marriages or marriages later in life will tend to have more separate property, since there is more opportunity for the partners to have acquired assets prior to the present marriage. Your attorney will put all this down on a spreadsheet to present to the other side.

If there is significant property involved in a divorce, or a marital home is at stake, you need to talk to your attorney about this early in the process. Make sure you understand the rules in your state regarding marital versus separate property, and the cut-off dates for this classification, particularly if you want to physically separate for a period prior to formally filing for divorce. In most situations, the parties can simply agree to a particular cut-off date for property. That is probably the easiest and fairest method, considering the peculiarities of each case and the fact that most cases will settle out of court.

Also, talk to your attorney if you need to document that something you brought into the marriage has, in fact, remained separate property, given the rules of your state. Remember, most likely you will be asked by your attorney to put together the details of what you consider separate and marital property, with supporting documentation. The attorney can summarize this information, but you need to come in prepared. This might involve a process of tracing the history of an asset during the marriage. That often takes a fair amount of time.

Active v. Passive Appreciation in Value

Now it becomes even more complicated. What happens if separate property or assets increase in value during the marriage? Is the increase in value separate property or marital? This raises another whole issue, the concept of active versus passive appreciation (or decrease). Passive appreciation is when separate assets increase in value due to things outside the control of the spouses. For example, suppose somebody had $100,000 in a Fortune 500 mutual fund prior to the marriage, they got married, and the mutual fund increases in value to $150,000 during the marriage because the stock market went up over the years, without the other spouse doing anything. The $50,000 increase is probably passive, and thus likely stays in the separate category. Increases in value due to inflation are also generally considered passive. For example, suppose one partner owns a rental house prior to the marriage, and this rental house increases in value over the marriage simply due to the inflation in real estate prices. The appreciation here is probably still separate. Of course, some assets can decrease in value, and generally the same concepts apply.

What makes an increase in separate property more marital in nature is activity to manage that asset during the marriage, or additional investments from marital funds to increase the value during the marriage. Actively managing a stock portfolio brought into the marriage might make the increase of the portfolio's value during the marriage a "marital asset" even though the initial portfolio value stays a separate property. Paying down a mortgage on the marital home, even if it was brought into the marriage as separate property, is probably a type of active appreciation, an appreciation of the net value of the house, since the payments made during the marriage probably came from wages earned during the marriage (which is marital). It can all get a little fuzzy, and there are a lot of gray areas, but the main ideas are clear.

For example, paying down a mortgage on a separate rental property, if the payments came from the rent, is probably itself a matter of separate property. But what happens if the rental house is actively managed by the non-owner spouse, or there are significant investments made during the marriage in fixing up the rental house above and beyond what would have normally been covered by the income received from rent? Then possibly it results in a bit of active and thus marital appreciation. All these issues need to be discussed with your attorney, and probably a good economics expert—but for now, just be aware of the differences between separate and marital property, and how they are viewed over the course of a marriage.

The passive versus active issue also becomes important when looking at what happens to the property after the separation. Assets that are primarily passive in nature, such as mutual funds and vacant land, will tend to be valued as of the date of trial—since nothing was done by the individuals to increase or decrease their value, their value depends on economic and market forces. However, assets and property that are considered more active in nature, such as a business or real estate where improvements are regularly made tend to be valued as of both the date of separation and the date of trial. Any active appreciation is then considered due to the separate actions by the individual managing it.

So, passive versus active appreciation tends to work in opposite directions, depending on the time frame. During marriage, active appreciation of a separate property is generally considered marital, while passive appreciation of separate property remains separate. However, after the separation (or cut-off date in your state), active appreciation, even of marital property, can be considered separate, while passive appreciation of marital property remains marital. It can be a bit confounding, but your attorney and financial experts will understand it.

Categories of Property and How They are Valued

Inevitably, assets and property within a marriage need to be accurately valued. This is true whether they are considered marital or separate as referenced in our discussion above. Generally, in cases of divorce, the standard for the value for any type of asset or property is called "fair market value." The term "fair market value" is defined as follows:

> *The price at which the property would change hands between a willing buyer and a willing seller, neither being under a compulsion to buy or sell and both having reasonable knowledge of relevant fact.*

Note that as previously mentioned, different states have different key valuation dates for purposes of divorce. Some states use the date of physical separation, other states use the filing or petition date for divorce, and yet other states use the "current date" or "date of trial," while some states allow the judge to have more discretion over the valuation date after hearing testimony. You need to make sure that you value or appraise your assets and property as of the appropriate date. If you value something, such as a piece of real estate, too far away from the appropriate valuation date, the court might discount your valuation and go with a value provided by your spouse that was determined as of a time closer to the official valuation date.

The first step is to categorize assets. These are the categories that I tend to use.

Bank Accounts, CDs, Gold Coins, and Cash: These are pretty straightforward; they have a cash value. $25,000 in the bank is worth $25,000. Gold coins, such as the U.S. American Eagle or the Canadian Gold Maple Leaf coin have a cash value you can look up. Thirty hundred-dollar bills in the family safe are worth $3,000. By the way, it's important that if you think a divorce is on the horizon, you should take dated pictures of any significant cash, gold coins, etc., that might be in the household safe. These have a very unusual way of suddenly disappearing.

Investments. A portfolio of stock is also fairly easy to put value on. Simply look up the market value as of the critical dates, such as the date of marriage or the date of separation or the key valuation date used in your state. Where a portfolio of stock becomes difficult is in the appreciation of the portfolio if part of the stock portfolio was brought into the marriage as separate property: then whether addition investments were made during the marriage (from marital funds), and/or the original portfolio has changed during the marriage due to the active management of researching, buying and selling stocks during the marriage can make a difference. In these cases, you will almost always need an expert economist or accountant to track or trace the history of these investments. This can be a daunting process even to an expert economist and it can take a significant amount of time to get the history straight to figure out the separate versus marital component. But if the portfolio is significant, this probably should be attempted. If it isn't a lot of money and the portfolio was managed over a long marriage, you should just consider it all marital.

Real Estate. Residential real estate needs to be appraised by a qualified real estate appraiser. However, for friendly negotiations and mediations, and for a residential property, it is sometimes possible to get agreement based on the values of various internet real estate sites, such as Zillow, Trulia, and Realtor.com. This is probably true of any residential property, whether it's your personal home or any single-family homes you might own that are rental properties. Remember, when it comes to real estate, some states view the "marital home" differently from other real estate investments in terms of the marital or separate property classification.

However, if you've made a lot of interior or exterior additions, upgrades, or if you disagree with the values obtained from these websites, then a real estate appraiser needs to be involved. Tax value is not a fair market value, and in some states cannot be used as a value in court. Also, if the divorce case can't be settled and it needs to go to court, or if the building is commercial in nature, or if the property is raw land, or a farm, then most certainly you will need to have a professional do the real estate appraisal.

Commercial real estate and multi-unit rental properties are different animals. In these cases, you should get a commercial real estate appraisal. Some commercial real estate appraisers might do a quick-look appraisal for small commercial properties, such as office condos, but for anything significant they will need to do a full analysis looking at the current economic conditions, the historical and future potential rent income, vacancy rates in the area, and other aspects of the market.

Cars and Boats: For cars, look up the values on the Kelly Blue Book, Edmunds, or CarFax websites. From our experience, this usually works fine. There are similar sites where one can get a pretty good estimate of the value of boats and jet skis.

Collections: Art, guns, coins and other collections are sometimes difficult to value, and at other times not. Whoever is the primary collector can probably get a good estimate, combining the purchase prices with looking up things on the various websites dedicated to collectors. Just be honest.

You can also have somebody else who has some experience and can act neutrally put a value on collections. I have done this for many collection items, such as vintage musical instruments, guns, military memorabilia, ancient Roman and Greek coins, watch collections, and signed art prints. The key thing is to document your source of value.

If the art or collection is very expensive or rare, then you might need a specialist appraiser. But remember, it can also be very expensive if you hire specialized appraisers. My suggestion is that if you can reasonably estimate the values of collectables using the web, it can probably work during the negotiations as long as you are being honest and can document these values. Even if it goes to trial, attorneys might suggest just stipulating to these values.

When fine art is involved, if the piece was recently bought at an auction, that is probably the fair market value. However, if the piece was purchased from a gallery or from the artist, the fair market value is probably a lot less. This is also true of jewelry. You can get it appraised if the jewelry is very significant but you need to realize that jewelry appraisers often give two different values: an insurance value and a fair market value (what it would sell for). You want the fair market value estimate, which is always lower. Most everyday jewelry doesn't need a formal appraisal. Just look up similar items on the web and lump them together.

Furniture and Household Items: Furniture, appliances, plants, and household knickknacks have some value. Don't use what you paid for them since these items depreciate in value quickly. Nor can you use the new price currently in a retail store as the fair market value for something used. Remember, used furniture, knickknacks and the everyday items that accumulate in any household are not very valuable, no matter how much you paid for them, or how much sentimental value they might have. Fair market value does not include a sentimental component. I would also include in this perspective various garage items, such as tools, athletic stuff, and exercise equipment. Don't stress out about this class of property.

People generally do a pretty good job in estimating the value of many of these items. Just be honest. Don't put a high or low value on household items when you really know it's not the true, fair market value. If you need to be more detailed, one option is to simply look at the original cost, then do a straight-line depreciation of 3 years, 5 years, 7 years, or 10 years, depending on the actual life of these items. The IRS has a depreciation schedule for different classes of business property. You can look it up and apply these tables to similar personal property. For example, computers use a 5-year deprecation. Thus, if you bought a home computer for $1,000 two years ago, you could use this 5-year depreciation. With a 5-year depreciation, every year the computer decreases in value by $200, so it would be worth only $600 two years later.

However, people can get completely ridiculous in this area. We have seen some divorcing couples spend hours and hours figuring out, and then arguing about, the fair market value of every item of the hundreds of items in their household, getting down to individual items such as coffee mugs, dog leashes, walking canes, electric shavers, and house plants (and yes, these are real examples). It's not a productive use of anyone's time. Focus on getting a fair and documented value for the big items and simply lump all the other stuff together.

Personal items: This category includes personal clothing and toiletries. And this is a book on humane and civilized divorce. Just let people have their personal items. You'll be a better person for it.

Life Insurance: If the life insurance is a "term" policy (where you are paying each month and are covered if you die, but there is no cash value accumulating with the monthly payments), it has no fair market value. If the policy is a "whole" life insurance, there is probably a cash value that has been accumulating. If the policy is a whole life policy, then call the insurance company or agent to learn the cash value.

Pensions: This is a tough one, particularly since divorcing spouses rarely want to give up any part of their hard-earned pensions. But if a pension, or at least part of it, was earned during the marriage, it needs to be valued and there will be a marital component.

There are essentially two types of pensions. The first type is called a defined contribution plan. This is where the employee and the employer contribute money in a defined amount or percentage of income (typically when the paycheck is cut) and these funds are then invested in some financial vehicle. These are often tax deferred, so a person only pays income taxes when the funds are taken out at retirement. 401(k) plans, 403(b) plans, employee stock ownership plans, and Simplified Employee Pension Plans or SEPS are the typical types of defined contribution plans. IRAs would fall into the same category, but generally only individuals contribute to an IRA.

Define contribution plans and IRAs are easy to value. They are worth what the investments are worth. There still might be an active versus passive, or separate versus marital component of these, as discussed, but the valuation is pretty simple: Look up the value on the monthly or quarterly plan statement, or online these days.

The second type of pension is called a defined benefit plan. This is a traditional plan where somebody gets a retirement amount based on a combination of their salary and the number of years worked. Many federal, state, and local government employees are covered under defined benefit plans. Many unions plans are of this type. Some corporate pensions are defined benefit plans, but many corporations have moved toward defined contribution plans in recent years. Military pensions are like a defined benefit plan, but military pensions are particularly valuable, since military retirement starts immediately after putting in the required 20 or

30 years. Most other defined benefit plans don't start until age 65 or so, depending on the plan. Many police and fire department employees also have different types of defined benefit policies.

For defined benefit plans, you need to hire an expert economist to value them. Every state has its own rules and key cut-off dates that define marital property, but in general to determine the value of a defined benefit plan the expert needs to figure out the present value of the future payments, considering when the retirement starts, such as age 65, and when it is likely to end, generally at the life expectancy of the covered person. This can become more complicated when somebody was already covered under a plan prior to the marriage. In this case, we again have a separate versus marital calculation. These calculations require expertise, and if it goes to court, you need to have an economic or financial expert present their findings.

One interesting problem in defined benefit plans is the idea of "vesting." Vesting refers to how many years you need to work before you can get an "ownership" right to your pension. Pension vesting is generally 5 years of work credit. Different states view the vesting issue differently. Some states might allow for a reduction of pension value if the person is not vested as of the date of separation or divorce, while other states basically say it doesn't matter if you are vested or not, the calculation must assume you are vested regardless. The expert really doesn't have a choice here. They must work within the statutes and case law of the state.

Understandably, the pension earner often wants to keep the full pension, even if it is technically considered "marital" in nature. But frequently, there are not sufficient other marital assets that can compensate the other spouse. In these cases, the parties can simply split the future pension payments appropriately, depending on the marital component. The court can issue a "Qualified Domestic Relations Order," or QDRO. This will order the pension manager to appropriately split the monthly pension payments, paying each person their proper share. The appropriate marital share is determined as of the date of separation and will not include additional years accrued after the divorce, or future promotions.

For military retirements, QDROs don't technically apply, since military retirement payments are not "qualified pensions" but rather a statutory entitlement by the U.S. government. Instead, the military applies their own formula which is very similar to the calculations used in QDROs but calculated as of the Date of Divorce. Military pensions are complicated, and the subject of entire books dedicated to explaining them.

Disability Payments: Disability payments, which are often paid due to a physical or mental (PTSD, etc) disabling event, can provide a source of income for a defined period of time, or in some cases, even a lifetime. Whether a specific type of disability payment is considered marital property and needs to be valued depends on the type of disability benefit, when the disabling event occurred, how the benefits are calculated, and the laws of the state. As with everything in divorce, there are a number of nuances and exceptions, but the following are some guidelines.

In general, there are four basic sources of disability payments. Social Security Disability Insurance (SSDI) payments are generally not considered marital property. However, in some cases, a divorcing spouse may be able to obtain some future payments under specific SSDI rules. The second type of disability payments are VA disability benefits. While military pensions can be divisible according to state rules, VA disability benefits are not considered marital property nor are they divisible. This is actually covered by Federal law. However, both SSDI and VA disability payments, while not considered marital property, can still be used to calculate child support and alimony.

The third type of common disability payments are from private disability insurance, such as what an employer might offer. These benefits can come from either short-term disability insurance or long-term disability insurance. Disability payments from private insurance can be considered marital, particularly if these payments are considered a replacement to lost income that would have been earned during the marriage. In these cases, your expert needs to calculate the present value of these future payments, almost like a pension. However, even this can be tricky, since some courts have argued that if the private insurance disability payments are to replace "lost future income capacity" rather than actual "lost income" during the marriage, then these payments might be considered separate property. Finally, workers' compensation settlement benefits are generally considered marital property and divisible, particularly if they are paid for lost wages and medical payments incurred during the marriage. However, if the workers' compensation is for future income loss that continues after the separation/divorce, then that portion might be considered separate property.

Businesses: If the marriage involves a business entity, then you need an expert—period. The next chapter addresses the complexity of business valuation. However, remember that in situations where one or both of the spouses are involved in a family business, this might also be the most valuable asset in the marriage. Very careful consideration needs to be given to this.

Really Complicated Assets: There are a variety of other types of assets or property that present complicated issues, even just to come up with a value. Fortunately, these types of assets tend to be rare in divorce cases. These might include long-term management stock options, convertible bonds, investments in an early-stage start-up firm, intellectual property such as patents or musical rights, annuities from an injury or insurance payment, condo time shares (which are not worth much), pre-paid benefits, personal loans made to somebody where it might be difficult to get paid back, and so forth. It can get even worse if somebody is a celebrity, professional athlete, or movie star. There might be an argument that even their name and celebrity status have value. If this is involved in your divorce, you will need to discuss with your attorney whether to call in an expert to value these things. Almost always, if an expert is required, it needs to be a specialized person who knows how to value these assets.

Sometimes during the marriage, a person might win a lottery, where the benefits are paid out over 20 years. Lottery winnings are generally considered marital. This windfall would be valued in a way similar to a pension.

Another confusing issue is a personal injury settlement that is either paid out over the years or as a lump sum. Generally, payments for pain and suffering, mental anguish, disfigurement, and other things that occurred due to an injury during the marriage are considered separate property, since a person's body is considered separate. However, payments to cover out-of-pocket expenses and compensation for a loss of income incurred during the marriage might be considered marital property. As always, different states have different rules regarding personal injury settlements and employment related lawsuits.

As a side note, if you are considering divorce while in negotiations for a personal injury lawsuit, talk to a divorce attorney to get guidance on how your personal injury attorney needs to make sure the settlement payments are recorded (such as payments for compensatory loss versus payments for pain and suffering) to keep them as separate versus marital property in your state. Many personal injury attorneys are not aware of how payments are categorized can influence whether these payments are considered separate or marital during a divorce.

We Might Work Things Out with Respect to Property

If there's nothing complicated about your property, such as no business ownership being involved, and all the property and assets are marital, then the wise, civilized, and humane approach is to try to value things yourself. Just make it simple. Yes, you might need to agree on a real estate appraiser for the marital home, but other things are probably not that hard. You can do this yourself. You also need to agree on a valuation date. Another good group of professionals you may want to consider in this case are called "Certified Divorce Financial Analysts," or CDFAs. I have worked with several CDFAs, and I think they offer a great service.

Basically, the underlying approach taken by a CDFA is to work with clients on the financial part of a divorce while keeping the price reasonable. The CDFA works with a divorcing couple to organize and categorize the financial assets. They can also assist the divorcing couple to develop a budget and to set post-divorce retirement objectives. CDFAs sometimes work with attorneys in providing the financial spreadsheet in a divorce case, or sometimes they just work with one or both spouses as a way of staying out of the court system. If you think your divorce is friendly enough to work through the property and other financial issues, and there is nothing really complicated, then definitely consider a Certified Divorce Financial Analyst. A CDFA can generally be found in most locations.

If you are working things out personally on the property side, just make sure you keep your attorney informed. They will probably encourage you to work things out, but your attorney will also provide a sounding board if they think you are being taken advantage of. Also, if you think you have an agreement with your ex, let your attorney look over the agreement before you sign anything. Emotions can run high, and sometimes you need a second set of eyes before signing any such document.

Final Comments About Property and Assets: The Net Value Rule

Remember that for divorce situations, we are talking about a "Net Fair Market Value." This means that if you value something, you need to subtract off any debt, mortgage, credit card payments, liens, and so on, to obtain a net value for purposes of dividing the assets. Thus a $500,000 home, with a $200,000 mortgage has a net value of $300,000—this is the key value.

Like everything else, states have different rules about debt. For example, some states specifically define gambling debts as separate. A few states have laws stating that a debt can't be assigned to somebody if they are not legally a signatory to the debt. Other states look carefully at excessive debt created during the marriage by one spouse, particularly if the other spouse was not aware of it. But in general, for most states, the debt incurred during the marriage, just like assets and property, is considered marital.

Dividing assets in a divorce situation means dividing them fairly, equitably, and according to the rules and laws in your state of residence. Almost always, this starts with the attorneys putting together a spreadsheet listing all the marital assets, their value, and who gets to keep them. If one side of the ledger is larger than the other, then there needs to be a transfer of funds or other assets to make sure they even out. Of course, there are also nuances even in this, depending on the state and whether it is a community property state or an equitable distribution state. But the spreadsheet showing the assets and their value, combined with any outstanding debt, and which party gets what after the divorce, will be the mechanism that the attorneys and judges use. The more individuals can assist in putting together this list, the less it will cost in attorney's fees.

Also, it's important to keep in mind that the division of property does not have to be equal, if one party feels like they are willing to accept less, or to give more. That can be fine. In fact, it might be the easiest way to settle or mediate a case. This is particularly true if there are disagreements about the value of certain property, or whether some assets are marital or separate. While the starting point always assumes a 50-50 split of marital property, often the best solution is simply to get an agreement that works for both parties. Fighting for the last percentage or two is simply not productive.

# Chapter 8

What If We Own a Small Business?

Now it Really Becomes Complicated

What if there's a business involved in dissolving a marriage? If this is the case, then suddenly the property settlement of a divorce has become a lot more complicated on many levels. If your family situation doesn't involve a business, then you can skip the next two chapters. However, if a business is part of the family, these are important chapters. Given that a divorce involving a business is more complicated, it's even more important that the parties understand the process.

In most marriages with a business, the business is the most valuable asset, along with the family house. Residential real estate is relatively easy to understand and value, but a business can be quite difficult. In addition, a family may have multiple businesses, with various family partners being involved differently. Businesses can also have outside investors and equity owners. And businesses may be immensely successful, generating a lot of family income, or they can be on the verge of bankruptcy. Some businesses have a lot of assets and inventory, like a machine shop, retail store, or wholesaler, while other businesses, like a consultant or doctor's office, may have few assets, relying more on their goodwill and reputation for success.

This chapter will be divided into several parts. We'll try to make a very complicated issue understandable so, when talking to your attorney, your experts, or even your ex-spouse, it all makes more sense. This chapter addresses the relationship between business and divorce in general. The issues in this chapter should be understood regardless of your personal involvement in the family business. The following chapter offers suggestions for the "business owner," the person who plans on staying with and running the business after the divorce. This person is often called the "in-spouse." We also provide recommendations for the "out-spouse," or spousal partner who will not stay with the business after the divorce.

It is important to understand that a business owned during the marriage is like any other asset in the marriage. As with real estate, cars, furniture, and investment portfolios, the business must be considered an asset of the marriage and addressed in the same way as other assets, according to the rules of your state. But unlike a house, car, furniture, or investment portfolio, figuring out the value of the business is much more complicated. It probably means getting experts involved. Because of this complexity, many times the situation with the family business is open to much more debate and disagreement than with other assets. Here are a couple of insights.

The Standard of Value

Like other assets involved in a marriage, the standard for the value of a business is called "fair market value." We discussed this in our property chapter, but it needs to be repeated and expanded here. The term "fair market value" is defined as follows:

> *The price at which the property would change hands between a willing buyer and a willing seller, neither being under a compulsion to buy or sell and both having reasonable knowledge of relevant fact.*

Definitions of fair market value used by various valuation and appraisal professionals have these common characteristics: (a) the buyer and seller are typically motivated but are not being forced into an exchange, (b) both parties are well informed and acting in their best interests, (c) a reasonable time is allowed on the market, and (d) there is a market for the asset. It is this standard that you should always use when thinking about the value of a family business. This is also the standard of value that the experts will be using. But unlike most assets, the fair market value of a business is found in its ability to generate future profit and cashflow. If not, then it's simply worth what the business assets can be sold for, less any debt and other obligations.

Who Owns the Business?

When we talk about a business in the marriage, we are referring to a business that is owned by one or both partners during the marriage. This ownership can be a complete, 100% ownership, or it can be a less than 100% ownership. Other persons not involved in the marriage, such as a parent, brother or just a non-related partner might own part of the business. Ownership of a business, however, is the key issue. If a person goes to work and only receives a salary (typically reported on a W-2 at the end of the year), this is not ownership. Ownership means that the marriage partner owns some form of private "equity" in a business, or some percentage of the business. An owner can also, of course, receive a salary from their own business. In this chapter, we are talking about a family business or "privately held" business. If the marriage owns a chunk of a publicly traded company such as IBM or Tesla, which is to say, the equity trades on the stock market, such as the New York Stock Exchange or NASDAQ, then the value is simply the stock price as traded. Family and privately held firms are much more complicated.

The Easy Part of Determining Ownership: Ownership of the family business can be determined in several different ways. The most obvious is when the company is formed as a corporation or limited liability company (LLC) within a particular state. In forming a private corporation, the owner has "equity" in that corporation reflected in shares. You can also look up the webpage of the state government office responsible for corporations, such as the Secretary of State. It's easy to check the formation date for any corporation, and to see the documents that have been filed with the State.

Normally, a privately held corporation will be an "S-corporation" which means that the taxes are filed in a way that the profit "passes through" to the owners' personal tax return (reported at the end of the year on a "K-1" form). An S-corporation files its annual Federal tax return on Form 1120S. However, some small family businesses might elect to stay as a "C-corporation." C-corporations file a Federal Corporate Tax return and pay corporate taxes. The owners then get a dividend at the end of the year. Many small family businesses are Limited Liability Companies (LLCs), in which the ownership is reflected as a "membership." In all these cases, it is pretty easy to identify ownership, the percentages owned by different partners, and the date of formation. This information should be on the tax returns.

Always remember, however, that the percentage of formal ownership in a business does not constitute marital ownership. One spouse might formally own 100% of the equity, but if the business was formed during the marriage, it is likely to still be all marital.

Many small family businesses, however, are not corporations or LLCs, but rather stay as a sole proprietorship, filing their taxes on Schedule C of their Federal Tax return. In addition, there are various professional partnership arrangements, particularly for professional practices such as attorneys and doctors. Most marriage partners will know if they "own" equity in a business, but not always. We are often approached by a spouse who thought their ex-spouse owned a business, but in fact they were only a salaried employee who worked as a high-level manager in the business and bragged at home about owning part of the business. On the other hand, in many cases, the ex-spouse might go to work at 8am and come home at 5pm, acting like they are employed, but they are actually paid as an "independent contractor" running their own business. The income from these independent contractors will be reported on Form 1099.

A person who is an independent contractor almost always is a "business" since they are not technically an employee. The only exception to this "1099" rule might be if the "1099" worker is treated completely like an employee but is paid as an independent contractor. An example might be a simple real estate agent who works for a larger franchise operation. But these exception cases tend to be rare and involve complicated legal issues that need to be discussed with your attorney if you, or your spouse, fall in this category of a "1099" worker.

Determining Ownership – The Rare Cases: In most cases the marriage partners will know whether they own a business, but it can become confusing in rare cases. There are rare situations when the courts may determine an individual owns a business when they don't have any obvious ownership. This could happen, for example, when a marriage partner has an option to purchase a business in whole or part. This is often called "constructive ownership." This option to purchase the business may be written or oral. An example might be an elderly non-related business owner who has decided that your spouse can "buy" their business sometime in the future and has written out an option purchase agreement. Another situation might be where a person might have "effective control" over a business. For example, suppose a mentally incompetent parent retired from the family business years ago, and your spouse, who is the sole heir, now completely runs the operations, making all the critical decisions. In essence, your spouse effectively "owns" the business, but they don't own any paper equity. These are rare cases but be aware and talk to your attorney about such situations if they apply.

The In-Spouse v. The Out-Spouse

The language used by attorneys and experts during a divorce is important. When it comes to a business, spouses are often referred to being either the "in-spouse" or the "out-spouse" by divorce attorneys. In most cases, but not all, one of the marriage partners is typically the primary person in the business. This is the one who gets up each day, goes to work, makes managerial decisions, and then comes home at the end of the day. This is the in-spouse. The in-spouse is also the one who is expected to retain the business after the divorce. Naturally, the in-spouse knows a lot about the daily operations of the business. This party typically has better access to financial records, and generally will have the loyalty of the office staff and other employees (although, not always). The out-spouse on the other hand is generally in a weaker position of knowledge since this spouse doesn't interact with the daily workings of the business.

An out-spouse may have very different levels of knowledge about the business. Sometimes, the out-spouse works in the business, and might have started the business together with the in-spouse, plus, they might have made important contributions to the success of the business or done the bookkeeping—but the out-spouse generally doesn't plan on retaining the business after the divorce. More often, however, from our experience the out-spouse really doesn't know much about the daily workings of the family business. These out-spouses might have had another job or have been busy taking care of the household or raising children, or they might simply not be interested in knowing anything about the business during the marriage. In some cases, the out-spouse has purposely been kept in the dark by the in-spouse, particularly if at least one of the parties knows or suspects a divorce is looming.

Depending on whether you are an out-spouse or in-spouse, your strategy to resolve the business issue in a humane manner will be different. There is a natural tendency for the out-spouse to want the highest value placed on the business, since they will get more other assets as compensation during the division of marital property. Not surprisingly, the in-spouse wants the lowest value applied to the business. Valuation experts know this tension, but a true professional expert will ignore these pressures and simply come up with their best estimate of the true "fair market value" of the business. But be aware of that fact that, unfortunately, many so-called business valuation experts can be influenced by the person for whom they work.

Sometimes spouses who both worked in the business think they can continue to own, and work in the family business after the divorce. It's rare, but this occasionally comes up. Most attorneys don't recommend this, and most judges will rule against it. It just seems a little odd; but if the partners can agree to it and not be dissuaded by the sound logic of the realities of divorce, it might work.

Picking a Business Valuation Expert

I have now valued well over 500 businesses, many for divorce cases, but also for buy-sell and investment decisions, estate and tax valuations, and commercial damage and insurance claims. The businesses have ranged from small "mom and pop" retail stores to professional practices to highly complex early-stage technology firms. I have also had the opportunity to review the reports of probably a hundred different business appraisers and experts in my career. The following comments are made from this perspective and only represent my experienced opinion.

How Do I Find an Expert? Many family law attorneys already have a favorite business valuator, particularly if they have been involved in many court cases involving businesses prior to your case. This does not mean that the attorney's choice or favorite expert is the best choice, by far. Often, your attorney will simply give you a contact number and reference, and you need to contract the business valuation expert. Other times your attorney will directly contract the expert.

Attorneys without much business experience will often ask other, more experienced attorneys in the region for their recommendations. Clients do have some say, since ultimately the client will pay the bill of a business valuator. In only a small number of cases does the actual client need to individually search for a business valuation expert on their own. If this happens to you, ask around, or possibly do a web-search. But then make sure you talk a bit with the person you initially contact. Remember, since a business is possibly the major asset involved in a divorce and is the area where there is probably the largest disagreement about value, everybody needs to be educated about this decision.

If your attorney seems a little unsure about business valuation, I strongly recommend that you ask them to read these chapters. There are certain things you need to look for in a business valuator or appraiser. Often, a spouse will find a business valuation expert through a google search. If you find somebody out of the region and willing to do a valuation for a low price, be very cautious. With all the accreditation societies popping up, it is easy to become "accredited" in business valuation, set up an internet business, ask a few questions about the business and financial statements, plug the numbers into a spreadsheet, press a button, and then generate a very attractive looking 30-page report. This unfortunately is becoming more and more common. Artificial intelligence (AI) programs are also starting to appear. True business valuation, however, is more about the nuances of the business and the market. It often requires talking through the complexities of how the business works, the past and future problems and opportunities, and how the industry and competition is changing. In many cases, the business valuator might need to physically come on site. And finally, if it goes to court, the business valuator may need to testify as an "expert." Be extremely careful of low priced, out of region business valuators even if they advertise "accreditation" and produce attractive looking reports. It's much better to stay regional and in person, if possible.

Key Success Factors for an Expert for a Simple Valuation: First, and foremost is experience in valuation. How many businesses have they valued? I would say it needs to be at least ten or twenty to have any type of real experience. Second, they need to be familiar with the court system and the laws of the state. Third, if there is any chance that your case will go to court, the expert you select needs to have been court qualified and testified in court in the past. I would say at least once, but the more the better. This question is always asked when an expert is being "qualified" in court: How many times have you previously been court qualified? Fourth, they need to have an economic, accounting, finance or business-related educational background. Fifth, they should have some knowledge or experience in the general type of business you need valued. And finally, it is preferable if the expert has run or at least worked in a real business other than their valuation business. This last key factor is important since a good valuator needs to understand the complex business issues you may raise on a personal level.

Key Success Factors for an Expert for Complex Cases: If your case is complex, you need to consider these additional critical key success factors. By complex, I mean that the case involves ownership in an early-stage company that is just starting up (perhaps even pre-revenue, such as many high technology start-ups); or in a company that is seeking investors and/or already has other private equity investors; or in a business that is undergoing transitions in the marketplace; a business that might not have accurate financial records; a firm with complex separate/marital components with significant appreciation during the marriage; any company going through acquisition discussions; a highly diversified company with many product or service lines; any company with international aspects connected to the business; and any type of valuation related to patents, copyrights, musical rights, or other components of intellectual property, such as trade secrets. In these cases, ninety-five percent of the professionals doing business valuation are simply not qualified to value such complex types of commercial activities. Given this, there is a good chance that an unqualified expert's testimony will be tossed out if it goes to court.

In addition to the basic key success factors mentioned above, there are other two major things you need to look for in an expert for these complex cases. First, does the person have an advanced graduate degree, such as a Ph.D.? These are complicated issues, and generally anything less than a Ph.D. in business or economics, or possibly in some cases, a good MBA degree, simply doesn't provide a sufficient educational background for completely understanding these complex issues. And second, the expert should have some personal experience in these areas. Experience comes in three forms. Have they personally been involved in these complex areas? Being able to understand the terminology and issues is key. Do they also have a specific background, such as in biology, information systems, music, or art, or at least taken courses in the areas related to the business at hand? And do they have some experience in valuing the activities in these complex areas? These types of experts are very hard to find, and you might need to search a bit for somebody perhaps even out of your local area.

Key Success Factors for an Expert if the Case is Going to Court:
Being a good business valuator does not mean the person can present their findings well in court. Quite frankly, judges are not business experts. Family law judges might have heard several business valuation cases, but they are not trained in the field. Most judges probably don't have an economics or business undergraduate

degree, although they do their best to understand. If the case is likely going to court, you need a valuation expert that has both court experience and a communication style of explaining complex issues in a simple, understandable manner. Both are requirements. I have heard horrible court testimony from very competent valuators. A good expert going to court can't just talk financial and accounting "gobble-de-gook," to use a professional term. Rather they need to be able to speak about very complex issues at a level understandable to the judge. And they need to respond carefully and correctly to tough cross-examination questions. Their communication skills are key.

Who Does Business Valuations? Essentially, there are three types of professionals who do business valuations.

1. University Faculty. These are the professors and faculty members who teach business valuation, small business management, accounting or finance at a university. Full-time faculty almost always have a Ph.D. in their field, they teach relevant courses in valuation and finance, and they publish articles in peer-reviewed academic journals. Most good faculty members are also encouraged to do consulting. This allows them to bring the best ideas and theories into practice, and it also gives the professor real-life experiences to bring back to the classroom. George Bernard Shaw is known for a commonly heard quote, "He who can, does; he who cannot teaches." While funny, it is absolutely not true for business school faculty, and probably not true for other university level professional schools, like Law and Medicine. Having worked in several top universities as a full-time faculty member, almost every business school faculty member I've known in my professional life has either started and run their own small companies, worked for years in larger corporations, or participated in a wide range of consulting, both domestically and internationally. Many faculty have done

all three. In fact, a broad real-life business background is often a pre-requisite for most business school job positions, in addition to a Ph.D., excellent communication skills, and top-notch research. However, while faculty members may have a better understanding of the deep theory behind valuation, you still need to make sure they have good practical experience with valuations. Unfortunately, many smaller communities may not have a regional university or college nearby.

2.   **Certified Business Valuators.** There are several certification organizations that provide training and certifications to folks who want to do business valuation. If you see a bunch of letters after a name not referencing an academic degree, then this is probably a certification. For example, I am a Certified Patent Valuation Analyst (CPVA), since I do a lot of valuation work in early-stage, entrepreneurial firms and with intellectual property. Generally, these certification programs only require an undergraduate degree, but they do provide their members with a good basic understanding of valuation methods. They also often offer templates for both the analysis and report, as well as access to certain databases. In my experience, these certification programs have dramatically improved the quality of general business valuation over the past thirty years, but the skill of the certified members varies tremendously in their ability to handle complex issues. In addition, while these certification programs may provide a good understanding of the basic valuation methods and members can all produce good looking reports (though mostly from cut and paste templates), they generally don't provide much understanding of the deep theoretical reasoning behind many of the valuation issues. That lack of deep knowledge may become obvious in a court hearing if the case is complex. But in most cases, these valuators do a competent job of business valuation..

3.   **CPAs, Accountants, Financial Planners, and Business Brokers.** These are professionals who work around businesses

all the time. Most of these experts have passed a certification requirement to enter their profession. Some of these folks have also taken special business valuation classes. They feel comfortable around financial and accounting issues, but business valuation may not be their specialty. I would say, for a preliminary cut or for issues that are fairly straightforward, if you already work with someone in these professions, get their opinion. Most likely, given their financial background and education, any judge will qualify them as experts.

How Do I Pick a Business Valuator? To answer this question, I like to use a medical analogy. If you have a simple cold or small cut on your finger, a nurse practitioner is perfectly appropriate. However, if your medical issues are more complex or serious, then you certainly want to see a physician that has both a medical doctorate degree and higher-level experience sets. The last thing you want is somebody not up to the problem. If you ultimately need surgery, you also want a doctor who has extensive experience in this particular type of surgery and can handle things under pressure. If your medical case is really complicated, then the best physicians are almost always going to be at hospitals associated with university medical schools. It's no different in the field of business valuation, or any other profession.

The bottom line is that a good business valuator requires a combination of two essential things: advanced education and experience. I would also add "ethics" to the list.

It's always important to remember that, unlike residential real estate appraisals, business valuations have an incredible number of assumptions built into them. How accurate are the financial statements? What should the discount rate be? What's a proper fair market salary adjustment? Are there non-working family members getting paid? How many personal items are being written off as business expenses? What impact does the current competitive situation have on the business? Is the economy going to get worse or better? Is a marketability or minority ownership discount appropriate? The list goes on. A small difference in any of these assumptions can make a big difference in the forecasted value. Most business valuators might disagree on these assumptions, but these are generally honest disagreements.

Unfortunately, from my experience, some business valuators can also be influenced by the person who hires them. By tweaking an assumption here and there, an "expert" can make a valuation high or low, depending on whether they are working for the in-spouse or out-spouse. I have seen it many times. It's painfully obvious, even with well-known valuation experts. In my own opinion, it's not ethical.

Personally, I tell everyone that my value is the same no matter who hires me. In fact, I often suggest that the parties agree to a joint valuation, since my valuation will be the same regardless. Occasionally, I have even withdrawn from a case when an attorney is putting pressure on me to determine a higher or lower value. I simply won't be influenced like this. Just be aware of how common this is. And the so called "codes of conduct" that many professional organizations promote really don't have much impact on ethical behaviors—there is plenty of published research to show this. Ethical behavior is a personal issue and it's important.

How Much Will It Cost? Most business valuators work on an hourly basis, generally with a retainer like an attorney. It's perfectly reasonable to ask the valuator how much time they think it will take, but that can be a hard question to answer. Some cases with accurate financial statements are relatively simple. Other cases can be extremely complicated and time-consuming. Oftentimes, the smaller "mom and pop" business will take more time simply because the financial information is often a mess, while larger firms may have professional accounting systems in place. But at least you might get a broad target cost. Prices are going to be higher in big cities. Be smart. Don't spend $20,000 on a business valuation for a business worth $40,000. Remember, not all businesses are valuable. Probably about 30% of the businesses I look at aren't worth much more than the assets they hold. They provide a decent income to the owner, but not much more.

Personally, I am very sensitive about the cost to the client, and particularly for clients with a small business in the marriage. For this reason, and since I also know that most cases will settle before getting to court, I do a shorter "quick look" valuation for purposes of settlement and mediation. This takes less time and is still pretty accurate. However, if the case goes to court, then I do a deeper dive (which generally means an analysis of the financial records, the general ledger, checking accounts, and credit cards) to be court ready. Normally, my "quick look" report value is pretty close to the "court-ready" report. By doing the "quick look" analysis first, I save the client a lot of money. I'm probably in the minority in doing this two-phased approach. Most valuators will do a court ready report up front and charge a lot for it. In my opinion, if you think the case will settle, then either agree to do a joint valuation, or ask your business valuator if they will do a less expensive, "quick-look" analysis.

What If My Spouse is Hiding Money? I teach a course titled, "Entrepreneurial Finance and Business Valuation" at my university and have seen literally thousands of small business tax returns in my career. In my opinion, probably at most, 5% are fully accurate. People always write off something, some more than others. In cash businesses, like small retail stores, restaurants, and coin operated laundries, generally most of the cash income is not reported on the tax returns. Business owners primarily do it for one obvious reason—to pay less tax. Other people are just sloppy at their record keeping. And some people do hide money from their spouses, in cash or in foreign bank accounts, as well as in other ways.

The starting point of any business valuation is the financial statements. A good business valuation expert can adjust the financial statements for typical things, like writing off personal expenses or personal cars, but if there are deeply hidden write-offs, or other funny things going on, you might need to hire a "Forensic Accountant" to look over matters. Forensic accounting is not overly complicated in theory, but it is extremely meticulous and detailed. It's a specialized area of accounting, and some CPAs are trained in this area. It is almost like an IRS audit. If you think your spouse is really playing games with the financial records, then you might need to hire a forensic accountant to investigate. These accountants are pretty expensive, however, and they put in a lot of hours, given the nature of their work. They should only be used when there are reasons to believe questionable stuff is being done on a major scale, and the business is worth enough to justify the expense. If not, just let the business valuator do their best.

Valuing the Business: What is Marital?

Unlike an investment portfolio, the courts generally don't split a business. Rather, the in-spouse will retain the business after the divorce but then needs to compensate the out-spouse for their marital share of the business. Normally this payment comes in terms of crediting the out-spouse with the appropriate value in real estate, other marital assets, or investments that the out-spouse will keep.

Here is where it can get quite complicated. Like any asset, the marital value of a business is broken down into various components. We will discuss the situation in equitable distribution (ED) cases, but there are similarities with community property states.

A business started during the marriage is considered all marital as a first cut. Just as if the parties were to buy a house, car, or furniture during the marriage. Take this as an absolute rule: Any business started during the marriage is considered "marital," unless one party can prove differently, and this will be possible only under certain circumstances. That accounts for most divorce situations involving a business, particularly for longer marriages. Note that it doesn't matter who started the business, who actually owns the stock in a corporation, whose name is on the legal documents for the company, who filed for the LLC with the state, who is on the business checking accounts, or who signs the contracts. If the business was formed during the marriage, there is a basic underlying assumption that it is marital. If somebody wants to prove otherwise (usually the in-spouse) the burden is upon that person and that individual's attorney, to prove it is not all marital. Note, however, that forming a corporation or LLC during the marriage does not necessarily mean the business started at this time. It may have been operating as a sole proprietorship for years prior to the formation of the corporation or LLC. This is one of the things that the in-spouse may argue, since if they can prove the business started before the marriage, the only marital component may be the active appreciation in the business during the marriage.

In cases where the business is all "marital", the expert in business valuation will appraise the business as of the date of separation or key cut-off date in your state for marital property versus separate property.

What Happens if the Business Was Started Before the Marriage?

Some businesses are clearly started before marriage. We often see this in shorter marriages. In these cases, in equitable distribution the only part that is generally considered marital (and subject to division during the equitable distribution process) is the active growth or appreciation in the business during the marriage. This means we need to look at two things. First, what is the growth of the business from the date of marriage to the date of separation/cut-off date? For example, suppose an expert determines that a business was worth $100,000 as of the date of marriage, and it was worth $300,000 as of the date of separation or valuation date. This results in an increase of $200,000 during the marriage. However, not all of this growth will be considered marital because it may not all be active growth. This is where it can get confusing, but it's exactly like any asset that we discussed in prior chapters.

The marital component in the growth of a business during the marriage is what is generally known as "active appreciation." This is the growth that is attributable to the activity of one or both the marital partners during the marriage. The other type of growth is "passive appreciation." The most common passive appreciation is just inflation, but it can also be caused by other things outside the control of the business partners, such as changing interest rates or market conditions. Passive appreciation needs to be taken out of the growth between the date of marriage and the date of separation, and what's left over is generally considered active appreciation. This active appreciation is the marital component for a business that was started prior to the marriage. So, if inflation counts for $50,000 of the $200,000 growth during the marriage in our example above, the active appreciation would be $150,000 (not $200,000). Thus the $150,000 is considered the marital asset. If there are other partners involved in the business, then it becomes even more complicated in teasing out the active contribution of just the person involved in the divorce. Your valuation expert will need to determine this, your attorney will need to argue it, and ultimately the judge will make the decision on this if it goes to court.

As we have mentioned, there are a small number of states that are considered "All Property" states, where having the business (or any other property) before the marriage doesn't matter—it's generally considered marital upon the date of the marriage. But even in these "All Property" states, the active and passive appreciation issues might matter, since judges have a lot of discretion regarding property distribution, particularly in shorter unions.

My Business Started During the Marriage, But It Was with Money I Inherited: In rare cases, business valuation can get even more confusing, particularly in equitable distribution states. Let's consider some of the even more complicated issues. First, like any asset, a business can also be inherited from a parent. In these cases, the business will likely be considered a separate asset, but any growth in the business due to active management of the spouse during the marriage will likely be considered marital.

But suppose the business was started during the marriage, but with money that was inherited by one spouse. This raises an issue known as the "source of funds." It's the same with other assets, such as buying a house or making investments. Inherited funds are generally considered separate assets. Likewise, a saving account that was put together by the in-spouse prior to the marriage is "separate." If these separate funds were used to start a business during the marriage, the in-spouse might be able to argue that even though the business started during the marriage, there is a separate component of it due to the "source of funds" argument. This is complicated, there needs to be a documented history, and you need to discuss it with your attorney.

Valuation and the Court Date

If you can't settle out of court, you might need to have a "Date of Trial" business valuation completed. Remember, equitable distribution states try to bring in a component of fairness to the property division decisions. What happens, for example, if the business has collapsed between the date of separation (or the cut-off date to define separate and marital property in your state) and the present time, like during the Covid-19 pandemic where many small businesses saw a massive drop in revenues, or simply went out of business. Business can grow or shrink between the date of valuation and the date of trial. This is particularly true given the overcrowding of the court system. There might be several years before the trial. In fact, we have done several cases where the property-related trial happened more than five years after the divorce, and the parties had gone their own separate ways. A lot can change in this time.

Suppose our example business above is valued at $300,000 as of the date of separation, and it is a construction business. But the housing market collapsed, and now the business is worth only $100,000. It is not very equitable to use the $300,000 figure to divide the assets, and the judge has some discretion. But this also means a valuation of the business will need to be done using data as close to the trial date as possible. In fact, many states require a date of trial valuation. In many equitable distribution states, the judge can use some discretion (based upon certain rules) to be "equitable". But even this is more confusing, since this is also a function of again, the notion of active versus passive appreciation.

If the business was worth $300,000 at the date of separation and the in-spouse used a lot of energy and skill after this date to help grow the business, then the growth of the business above $300,000 might be considered separate—after all, it was that spouse's personal activity and effort after the date of separation that grew the business. But as we have mentioned, if you live in a state where the cut-off date for marital property is the filing for legal separation or the filing of the court petition, this growth might be considered "marital" if it occurred prior to this cut-off date, but "separate" if it occurs after this cut-off date.

And yet, suppose the growth (or decline) of a business is completely out of the control of the in-spouse, as in the case of the Covid-19 pandemic. In these circumstances, the judge might consider this change in value more "passive." It's the same as with other investments, such as a stock portfolio that the parties haven't touched or actively managed. Whew, it can be confusing, but it is important to understand these complexities when talking with your attorney and experts.

These decisions are generally under the jurisdiction of the judge using the rules set forth in their state. But this is why your business expert may need to do three or four different business valuations—

one for the date of marriage, one for the date of separation, one for the state's official cut-off/valuation date, if different, and one for date of trial, as well as compute passive versus active appreciation between these dates. It sounds complicated, and it is, but it really comes from trying to be as fair as possible during divorce and property division decisions. But as we have mentioned several times, the parties can agree to simplify the process and agree to a certain date for the valuation, particularly if they believe the case will settle. And above all, try to settle the whole business issue, perhaps with the help of the experts preliminary valuations and insights, before going to court and it gets even more convoluted and expensive.

Additional Obligation If the Business Is a Corporation/LLC

Almost everything we have discussed so far is covered under the laws governing divorce and marriage within a particular state. However, a business can add an additional component of complexity in a divorce situation if they are a corporation or LLC. Forming a corporation brings a lot of advantages, such as limited liability, but it also brings obligations – the same basic obligations as Fortune 500 firms that are also corporations. Many people forget about these obligations.

For example, suppose that a corporation is formed for your small business during the marriage, and that the marital partners each get 50% stock ownership in the corporation. One partner makes themself the "President" and the other spouse becomes the "Vice-President." But then consider another case in which a corporation is formed during the marriage, but the in-spouse formally takes 100% of the corporation's stock yet, as above, one partner makes themselves the President and the other spouse becomes the Vice-President, even though the Vice-President doesn't legally own the stock.

From an equitable distribution/divorce process both business-es are still all marital, as discussed above, since they were both formed during the marriage. However, once a corporation (or LLC) is formed, there is a whole new set of responsibilities under the rules of being a "corporation". This can become a confusing situation since many family law attorneys are not overly familiar with corporate law. This issue generally comes into play in two areas, the idea of "fiduciary duty" and what is known as "share-holder freeze-outs".

In the case where each marital partner formally owns 50% of the stock, the in-spouse (who is likely the President of the com-pany) has a "fiduciary duty" to the other shareholder (the other spouse). This fiduciary duty means that the President needs to act in the best interest of all the shareholders, and not just in their own-self-interest. This generally involves three duties: 1) a duty of care (making business decisions even during a divorce in good faith), 2) a duty of loyalty (putting the interest of all shareholders above their own self-interest), and 3) a duty of good faith (not having an intentional dereliction of duties).

In addition, many states have "shareholder freeze out" laws. These rules basically state that a person who owns a large percent-age of stock (generally over 30% or so) has a "reasonable expecta-tion" of having a job in that business, etc. Why is this important?

Most divorces are not overly friendly, and the in-spouse Pres-ident might "fire" the out-spouse from their Vice-President's job, lock them out of the office, and change the checking account. While it doesn't change the marital issue, if the out-spouse doesn't formally own any stock, this might be fine from a management point of view. However, if the out-spouse has a 49% technical equity ownership in the corporation, this might present some big problems under corporate rules since that is a classic "sharehold-er freeze out". In addition, corporations need to have shareholder meetings, board of director meetings, and follow other rules, so major decisions, such as "firing" the ex-spouse, should be done according to the corporate bylaws, etc. Just make sure you make your attorney aware of these issues. There are ways of addressing them within a family law setting.

I find that many divorce attorneys often forget the corporate law aspects in a divorce involving a business. But I have worked on domestic cases where corporate fiduciary duties have played a critical role in how the judge ultimately decided to award the property.

In addition, if there are other outside investors, they may not be overly interested in your divorce, but they do want to protect their ownership in the business. And believe me, if these outside investors think you are diminishing the value of their investment because you don't like your spouse, you will likely get sued at a later date. Bottom line, if you have a legal business entity, like a corporation or LLC, be very careful about your actions during a divorce, and always talk to your attorney about these issues, whether you're the in-spouse or the out-spouse.

Chapter 9

PROPER BEHAVIORS OF THE BUSINESS SPOUSES

Treat the Business Respectfully

This chapter provides specific recommendations for both the out-spouse and the in-spouse in a business. Both parties should realize that fighting over business value is generally not productive. Court costs are high, the attorney's and expert's time are valuable, and generally when it comes to the marital business, the judge will likely come up with a value that is probably close to what could be achieved through honest negotiations and mediation. However, being informed is a key element to this process.

A starting point for this chapter is the notion of the humane, a key theme for this book. As discussed in the opening chapters, humaneness historically has several elements. One element discussed in the Biblical Book of Wisdom is that an individual should be informed about the situation. However, another important element of humaneness lies in the notion of compassion, sympathy, and consideration—the outcomes of true empathy. Divorce, by its nature, is an ugly process with high emotions. Other than child custody and spousal support, from our experience, the biggest fight about property often focuses on the family business. But understanding how to address the marital asset of a business must be kept in the realm of the humane.

Thoughts for the Business Out-Spouse

Recommendation 1: First and foremost, the out-spouse needs to understand the emotions of the in-spouse when it comes to the business. Starting a business has been likened to a birthing process. The entrepreneur invests not only financial assets in a start-up, but large amounts of time, effort, and a range of emotions. Starting and growing a small business is not easy, and many businesses fail. The owner needs to sell their product or service in highly competitive markets. The owner must deal with shoddy suppliers, problem employees, and financial downturns. They almost always work extremely long hours. Starting and growing a business can be far more stressful than a 9-to-5 job.

A successful small business becomes almost like a child to the founder. A divorce, by its very nature, has the potential of tearing this all apart. Not surprisingly, the in-spouse will always act defensively, not only to protect their personal financial aspect, but also to protect their life investment and emotional investment.

It is very important that the out-spouse has a bit of empathy here. It is perfectly correct to expect fairness but you should also be careful about such statements as, "I'm going to destroy your business." Remember that the family business is almost like another family member to the in-spouse. And there may be other employees who work in the business, where the business is the source of their livelihood as well.

Also, if the in-spouse's business is the primary source of family income, and you, as the out-spouse are expecting alimony, child support, and other spousal assistance, you really want the business to be successful in the future, since that will be the source of much of this assistance. Just be sensitive to what you say and do.

Recommendation 2: Since founders and entrepreneurs treat their small business almost like raising a child, they also tend to brag about their success, or cover up their failures. Don't be surprised if you have been told around the dinner table how great the business is, when in reality it's nowhere near as profitable as you might think. For example, I worked on one case where the out-spouse was told for years by the entrepreneur that they were millionaires, rolling in cash, when in fact the family business was on the verge of bankruptcy, and did go out of business after the divorce.

Just be aware of this natural tendency for the entrepreneur to be somewhat proudly optimistic and enthusiastic about their business in conversations. What your spouse says the business is worth when you are happily married is probably not true (too high), and likewise what the spouse says the business is worth after a separation is also probably not very true either (too low). Remember, there are always personal motivations at stake when people talk casually about their business.

Recommendation 3: Become knowledgeable about the business. Spouses should be familiar with the family business even if they are not getting divorced, but it's even more important if the marital partnership is falling apart. Make sure you learn about the business before separating or filing for divorce. The more you know about how the business works, what the in-spouse does in the business in a fair amount of detail, how many hours they work in the business, and the opportunities and threats for the business, the more you can provide your valuation expert and attorney with this important information.

Your attorney and valuation expert will certainly ask you these questions when they interview you. This is probably the biggest problem in working with out-spouses: They should be much more informed about the family business. So often we hear, "I really don't know anything about the business." This starts the valuation process on the wrong foot.

Recommendation 4: Get financial data about the business before separating. The valuation of a business must be based on financial data, and the starting point will always be historical data. Your attorney will certainly ask for this information in a formal request, but before filing for separation or divorce, try to obtain at least three years of financial records. It's far easier to acquire this information well before separating or filing for divorce. This would include tax returns as well as internal financial statements. Make sure you get a list of the equipment owned by the business. And if possible, get a copy of the general ledgers, for at least 2 years—this can be in hard copy, or electronic copy if the business uses a software program like QuickBooks.

Also, understand what debt has been incurred that is truly business debt. Sometimes people will borrow money to buy a boat, for example, and then try to say it's for the business. Make an effort to understand not only the revenues, expenses, and profit of the business, but also its assets and liabilities. It's a lot easier to get this information early, rather than waiting for responses from a court order and after you've been locked out of the business.

Recommendation 5: Was there an offer to purchase the business in the past? If the firm has received a bona fide offer of purchase in the past couple years, get the documents—e-mails, letters, formal offers, and so on. Remember, however, that many small business owners brag about being approached to sell their business for big money, when it was just wishful thinking.

Recommendation 6: If you have applied for a home or business loan, get copies of the documents. Many times, the loan documents will ask the entrepreneur to put a value on their business for the loan. It may not be accurate, but it might be important for your attorney to see.

Recommendation 7: What's the accuracy of the financial statements? We all know that most tax returns filed by small, family businesses are probably not very accurate. Almost everybody writes off personal expenses as a business expense. Some do it more aggressively than others. Nearly everybody writes off phones, cars, entertainment, and such, but we have also seen very aggressive write-offs, like trips to Europe, professional football tickets, all the personal family shopping trips, pleasure boats, sports cars, renovations to the family home, and on and on.

The reason small businesses do this is obvious—nobody likes to pay taxes. But in approaching a divorce, it is very important that you have a pretty good idea about how aggressive these write-offs have been. The more detail you can compile about what is being written off and how much, the better off you are.

Your attorney and valuation expert will almost always ask about these write-offs, and you need to have some good answers. The more examples you can find, the better. However, just because you and your spouse have been charging personal things on the company credit card, or writing company checks for non-business purchases, it doesn't mean they're being written off as business expenses. It could be that the business accountant or bookkeeper is recording these purchases as an "owners draw," which is perfectly fine. However, if these items are being written off as a "business expense," the more documents you get to prove it, the better. Also, if you believe the business tax returns border on fraudulent, make sure you tell your attorney, since they might be able to deal with potential IRS complications during a divorce settlement.

Recommendation 8: A "cash business" presents a special problem. In small businesses like non-franchised family restaurants, single person renovation and contracting operations, lawncare firms, coin-operated businesses, antique shops, and other types of small retail shops, a lot of cash typically is brought in. "Cash" can also be in the form of checks written out to the person, rather than to the business, or in the modern world of electronic payments, with the use of Venmo or other payment services.

Not surprisingly, this cash is not often declared or reported on tax returns. You can't tell your valuation expert, "Oh we also take in a bunch of cash." Your statements about this, even if true, are simply not sufficient for the valuation expert or attorney. You need to prove it with a second more accurate set of books, a list of cash receipts for the year, cash deposits in a separate family account, or pictures of cash taken in each week—proof of non-declared cash receipts is critical for it to be used. Just get something to back up your belief. If there's no proof, your valuation expert probably can't use your statements.

Recommendation 9: Some business accounting is so bad that the financial statements and tax returns are simply useless. They're useless because of either horrible bookkeeping or intentionally falsifying tax returns. In this case, the valuation expert may use a "lifestyle" approach as a last resort to figure out how much profit the family business makes. This method is like the "lifestyle audit" used by the IRS. I can't tell you how often we see tax returns reporting a small $30,000 income, yet the family lives in a $600,000 house, drives new cars, and regularly goes on vacations to the beach. The math simply doesn't work.

Basically, when using a lifestyle approach, the valuation expert needs to calculate how much money your family spends on all your household expenses—rent or mortgage, insurance, utilities, car payments, gas, food, clothing, kids' books, entertainment, trips, savings, etc. There are literally a hundred different things a family might spend money on each month. These funds must come from someplace, and if the family business is the only source of income, then it must all come from the profit and income of the business.

A lifestyle approach involves writing down with proof your monthly family expenses. If you're thinking about separating, and you feel your spouse's business financial records are really bad, then start recording your monthly expenses: write them down in a log and get proof for the past several months in the form of receipts, bills, and canceled checks. This may be the only way of proving your family business was making good money and therefore has some value. You'll need several months or a full year of fairly accurate records. From my experience, the life-style method is not used much, but is necessary some of the time as a last resort.

Thoughts for the Business In-Spouse

As discussed before, fairness and knowledge are key to a humane divorce. This attitude also needs to underline the in-spouse's approach to the business valuation process.

Recommendation 1: Don't tell your attorney or valuation expert that you "are the business" and it therefore has no value. We hear that all the time, probably in 95% of our initial interviews. A good valuation expert knows a lot about many different types of business. We also know that individual effort, plus a little bit of luck, is what really builds a small business. But always remember that the value of any business is its ability to generate income in the future.

It might be surprising, but very personal types of businesses are sold every day, and there is often a fair market value associated with these types of businesses. Personal types of business do have a lot of what is called "personal goodwill," or the ability to personally interact with customers and clients. The valuation expert will take this into account. In addition, a divorce is a unique situation, and a little different from just selling a business on the open market. In a divorce situation, there is already a market for your business—the market is you, the in-spouse. Since the in-spouse is normally retaining 100% of the business after the divorce, essentially the in-spouse is repurchasing (on the spreadsheet) the out-spouse's marital component of the business and its ability to generate future income.

Recommendation 2: Don't purposely try to decrease the value of business, thinking that will help you in the divorce process. Reducing revenues and decreasing profit is a bad strategy for three very important reasons. First, people will look at the business situation as of the date of separation. Second, if you purposely hurt the business, you might be accused of "wasting a marital asset," which is the same thing as smashing a family car or burning the family house down. And third, it may be difficult to recover those lost revenues in a competitive market.

Recommendation 3: Don't play games with the business ownership. Some business owners actually believe they are smarter and cleverer than the attorneys and valuation experts. Take this as an article of faith: we have seen all the tricks.

The most common trick is starting a second company under a different name after the separation, then moving new customers to the new business, claiming the old marital company is now dying. Another trick is "selling" the business at an artificially low price to a friend or family member with the intention of "buying" it back after the divorce, then claiming the low sales price is the value. Another is to "hire" friends and family members, then pay them a big salary which flows back to the owner but decreases the reported profit. You should understand that attorneys and valuation experts are aware of all these methods. A good valuation expert has also probably run their own business sometime in the past, so they know how businesses work. These types of tricky manipulations of the truth are truly counterproductive. They rarely work, they'd show you to be dishonest, and the courts ultimately don't like such tricks.

Recommendation 4: Be forthcoming with requested documents. If the opposing attorneys ask for documents, and they will, just give them up and get it over with. The document request list for marital businesses tends to be extensive, and it might be a hassle. But it's better for all involved to just provide the information and get that part done. Tell your bookkeepers, your accountants, and your office staff to be cooperative. Not providing all the requested documents simply extends the process, costs more in terms of attorney fees, and upsets people whose goodwill you might need.

Recommendation 5: Keep good records. You should always do this, regardless of whether there are marital problems. This is particularly true if you are a corporation or LLC. Make sure you have your board meetings, keep minutes, and follow all the processes described in your corporate or LLC bylaws. Asking for corporate records is almost always on the document request list from the opposing attorneys and not having these can show a degree of bad faith in being a corporation or LLC. Remember, nobody really cares about whether you hold annual shareholder meetings and keep minutes for a small family corporation or LLC until there is a problem, and that's when they become very important. Just follow the rules, and above all don't create fraudulent or backdated documents. And don't forge your ex-spouse's name on anything. Being shown that you committed forgery never comes across well in front of a judge.

Recommendation 6: The fair market value of any business is its ability to generate profit and cashflow in the future. Valuation experts, however, use historical financial records such as tax returns, to help them predict the future income. If you had a great year in the recent past, something that's extraordinary and not likely to be repeated in the future, make sure you let your valuation expert know this. But also make sure you can support your claims, such as showing a large one-off contract that will not be repeated. Also, if the future is going to be different from the past, like Walmart moving into the area that will take away a big part of your retail store's business, get the proof and pass it on to your valuation expert. This proof can be an announcement in the paper, but the key is to support your statements.

 # Chapter 10

Pre-Nuptial Agreements and Post-Nuptial Agreements

The Oddities of Nuptial Contracts

In some cases of divorce, there are pre-nuptial agreements or post-nuptial agreements. These agreements are aimed at resolving property and support issues between either prospective spouses or else between spouses before a marital dissolution. By definition, prenuptial agreements or documents are signed prior to a marriage. Postnuptial agreements are documents signed after the marriage. The purpose of these agreements is almost always designed to address the division of property and assets. At first glance, nuptial contracts might seem a little odd for a happy marriage, but sometimes they make sense.

Purpose and Frequency of "Pre-Nups"

Unless one or both spouses are very rich or famous, prenuptial agreements are actually fairly rare. They tend to be more common in cases of second or third marriages, and when there are substantial assets and property belonging to one party prior to the marriage. We rarely see prenuptial agreements being executed prior to a first marriage, unless there are some unusual aspects of the property that one spouse owns, or if you live in one of the few "All Property" states.

The purpose of a prenuptial agreement is primarily to protect a spouse with significant assets that they acquired prior to the marriage. Prenuptial agreements are also used to protect these assets in a way that is different from the normal equitable distribution or community property laws of the states in effect when going through a divorce.

What is both interesting, and somewhat depressing, is when these agreements tend to pop up. We often find that the discussion of prenuptial agreements tends to enter the conversation only a couple weeks prior to, and sometimes only days before, a scheduled marriage. In these cases, it's often presented as a "done deal" by one person, and that the other person is almost forced to execute the agreement. The bewildered soon-to-be spouse is often left feeling that there is little choice but to sign the agreement if he or she wants to go through with the marriage. In fact, the condition of marriage is often attached to the execution of the prenuptial agreement. And this can be a shock to the recipient of such a document, however it's explained.

Certainly, one of the major and most acrimonious issues in a divorce situation is the division of property. There is certainly nothing wrong with attempting to avoid any potential future misunderstandings prior to marriage. It might in fact be a good idea to rationally, honestly, and thoughtfully discuss property issues well in advance of the marriage. But, as is said in the old expression, "There's a time and a place for everything."

We're always surprised when these agreements are presented so close to the marriage, and especially when they are delivered as an "either-or" edict. Often, the fact that the day of the ceremony is soon upcoming, the venue is ready, catering is arranged, guests are excited to attend, and other emotional and financial investments have been made is used as pressure to obtain quick compliance and signatures. This is probably not a good indicator of a healthy future relationship.

How Courts View Prenuptial Agreements

Prenuptial agreements are contracts, and there is an assumption that spouses have signed these agreements as willing and rational individuals. That is generally how the court looks at them. However, the execution of the prenuptial agreement is subject to some scrutiny, although it is rare that such agreements are simply set aside.

A prenuptial agreement can be subject to extreme scrutiny if it's completely one-sided and if it appears to have been thrust upon a spouse only a day or two before, or even the evening prior to, the marriage. This happens more often than most people might think. In addition, as a contract, prenuptial agreements need to follow the rules of a proper contract. If the prenuptial agreement fails at the contract law level, courts might indeed set it aside.

More commonly, however, prenuptial agreements are simply incomplete. They might cover a couple of the important aspects of property settlement but completely miss other vital aspects. In these cases, the courts will enforce what's included in the agreement but then let the laws of the state cover what's missing in it, unless your prenuptial agreement has waived that right, which they often do.

What we often see missing from these agreements are the important and somewhat complicated aspects of what defines separate and marital property, especially if a business is involved. This is particularly true if there are multiple businesses and investment properties that are actively managed during the marriage. And it becomes even more complicated when there are unusual characteristics of value brought into the marriage, such as the ownership of patents, copyrights, music or film residuals and other intellectual property that one partner is continuing to work on or promote in order to develop this property further in the future.

For example, an individual might have developed an invention and filed for a patent before the marriage but then continues to develop the idea beyond the specifics of the foundational patent. Or what if part of a potentially best-selling novel is written prior to the marriage, but then completed during the marriage? Then, of course, for celebrities, sports stars, and movie actors, there is also value in their own name or celebrity status. These are highly complicated issues that require true legal expertise to either write a proper prenuptial agreement or to challenge one in court.

In this book, we have to consider the issue of pre-nuptial agreements from two positions. If the spouses cooperatively agree to a prenuptial agreement well before the marriage, without any time pressures or its being forced on one spouse at the last minute, then the agreed-upon conditions may be perfectly fine, and it just needs to be properly worded. Prenuptial agreements generally have several goals that the spouses are trying to achieve. However, if a prenuptial agreement is in place and marriage is dissolving, the opposing party (and their attorney) needs to understand where a prenuptial agreement can be challenged. It's all in the wording.

Having reviewed, written, and challenged many prenuptial agreements, the following are my suggestions.

What a Prenuptial Agreement Should Cover

A good and effective prenuptial agreement should cover several important factors.

1. Don't Reiterate State Laws. A good prenuptial agreement should not simply restate what the laws of the state have already defined. We have discussed many times in this book that both equitable distribution and community property states view property and assets brought into the marriage pretty much the same way. The differences are subtle, and your attorney will know these differences. But in general, with the exception of "All Property" states, any property that you owned prior to marriage remains separate unless you purposely transfer title to that property to your spouse. And any property acquired as a gift or inheritance during the course of marriage is also separate property. A well-written prenuptial agreement shouldn't just repeat what the law already covers, but it should refer to the key aspects of the law in your state.

2. Make an Inventory of Separate Assets. While individual states have well-thought-out laws about property and assets, a good prenuptial agreement needs to take an inventory of the important assets being brought into the marriage so there is no confusion later. This should be done for each spouse. A good prenuptial agreement should delineate what that property is and have exhibits attached to the prenuptial agreement. Debating whether something is separate or not is a confusing, time-consuming, and expensive proposition during a divorce. And even with a prenuptial agreement, this is often the major point of contention: Is the property covered under the "prenup" or not? This is particularly true if the property or assets are not clear in nature, such as patents, intellectual property rights, celebrity status, etc.

3. Address Separate Property During the Marriage. A good prenuptial agreement needs to address what happens with originally separate property during the course of the marriage. Property can be brought into the marriage as separate property but can be easily converted into marital property by very simple acts, such as titling real estate in joint names, co-mingling assets, or even letting your spouse regularly "use" an asset, depending on the rules in your state. In fact, this transferring to the marital estate may not be the

intent of one party, but it does happen, sometimes out of igno-
rance of the law, sometimes based on the recommended actions
by third parties, and sometimes even by one spouse aggressively
demanding certain things during the marriage that result in a legal
gifting. This happens much more than people think. For example,
we often hear the pressures of one spouse to have the other spouse
put their name on a property title they brought into the marriage
if they "really love" them—then one year later that spouse files for
divorce. In addition, transfers of deeds are often done at the behest
of mortgage brokers when refinancing a home brought into the
marriage by one spouse. Both spouses are often required to sign
the refinanced loan documents for the property. It is generally not,
however, a requirement that both spouses be placed on the deed.
But we find that couples are often advised by some mortgage brokers that this is necessary to effectuate a new loan.

The rules regarding this can vary from state to state and between
lending institutions. This often creates tremendous problems at
the end of a marriage, particularly in a short-term marriage. By
these actions, a large portion of one spouse's separate estate could
be quickly transferred to the other spouse by title. While there
are some arguments for an unequal distribution of the estate, if it
came from largely separate sources (particularly in Equitable Distribution states), it is rare that judges move off a 50-50 split if the
asset or property appears to have been jointly titled during the
marriage by what appears to be a voluntary action by both parties.

4. Address the Appreciation of Assets. Another issue in a
pre-nuptial agreement is to address the issue of appreciation of
assets, whether personal or business in nature. We have talked
about the important issue of appreciation of assets in other chapters, but a prenuptial agreement should also address this issue.

A good example of active appreciation is when a married couple
pays down a mortgage on a piece of property during the marriage.

Let's say one party brings a personal residence into the marriage that has a $300,000 mortgage. The married couple live in the residence, and during the marriage the mortgage principal is reduced to $100,000. This paydown of $200,000 is a form of active appreciation, since it involves active participation by the parties, probably with funds earned during the marriage.

Another example is in the case of a business, where efforts by either spouse has grown the business during the marriage. The active appreciation of the business value is also marital.

Basically, efforts to enhance the value of separate assets, or further investments into separate properties during the marriage, are generally determined to be active appreciation and therefore marital property. An effective prenuptial agreement can make it very clear that any appreciation attached to a piece of property or asset, whether real estate, a business, or investments, whether it is active or passive appreciation, will remain the separate property of the person who owned it prior to the marriage. This addresses the main concern that any spouse would have over the increase or decreases of a separate asset during the marriage.

5. A Waiver of Rights to State Rules. A good prenuptial agreement should provide for a waiver of rights to divide your property according to the state rules, whether it is an equitable distribution or a community property state. A good prenuptial agreement will not simply leave that issue silent. If it is left silent, then neither party will truly know whether they have waived rights to a division of assets at the date of separation or divorce. That waiver of the division of assets upon separation needs to be clearly stated in a prenuptial agreement.

6. Inclusion of a Waiver of Other Rights. What is often left out of prenuptial agreements, even after the parties have agreed on what will remain separate property and a waiver of state rules to distribution, is a plan by the parties for the division of their assets upon their subsequent separation. The lack of any guidance about how assets will be divided leaves the parties open to potential litigation and/or interpretation by a judge as to whether there's been a proper waiver or not. I find that the simplest way to address this issue is as follows. Put another provision in the prenuptial agreement that simply and clearly defines the division of assets. As an example of this, the provision could state that anything belonging to the husband prior to the marriage and still in his name at the time of separation, would go to him. Likewise, anything owned by the wife and still in her sole name at the time of separation, will go to her. If the parties, however, choose to jointly title any piece of property, either in the form of joint bank accounts and or real estate, that property will be divided evenly between the parties. While this may seem to defeat somewhat the purpose of a prenuptial agreement, it does provide guidance with regard to how to divide assets upon separation. Most importantly, it also leaves the division of property in the couple's hands during the marriage. In other words, it will be a joint decision as to whether property acquired while married will be held jointly by the parties or not. To put it another way, it provides that in this respect the future is totally under the married couple's control.

7. *Waiver of Support.* Prenuptial agreements will often include a waiver of spousal support clause. In many states, there are prohibitions on the level of waiver of support. This is to prevent a completely dependent spouse from being left in poverty after the divorce. However, an agreement to waive support in the form of either temporary alimony, alimony, or post separation support is valid if addressed and executed in a prenuptial agreement according to state rules.

8. *Death of a Spouse and a Will.* Prenuptial agreements should also contain waivers by either party with regard to their respected estates upon death of one of the spouses. In most states, on getting married the parties become automatically intertwined with regard to finances and property. Upon the death of one of the spouses, there are certain rights the surviving spouse has to collect against the estate even when they are left out of the will. The right to a portion of an ex-spouse's estate upon their death differs between states and is beyond this book. Just be aware that it exists in many states in different forms. A solid prenuptial agreement should include a waiver of all those rights. It should also include a provision that allows either party to execute a will, leaving property to whoever they want. This leaves control of the disposition of the estate to the parties during the course of the marriage.

9. Retirement and Pension Rights. A good prenuptial agreement will also include a specific waiver of any retirement and pension rights. This is to make it clear that neither party is gaining in the interest in the other party's retirement as it accumulated during the marriage. This is important since in most instances an increase in the pension or retirement value during the marriage is in fact, marital property.

10. Disparities in Wealth. If there is a gross disparity in wealth, I always suggest that there is a specific clause in the prenuptial agreement that specifies some type of financial renumeration for the disadvantaged spouse.

11. Trigger Points in the How Much Remuneration. The prenuptial agreement can also address the issue of financial remuneration to the spouse after a certain number of years of marriage. As an example, if the parties have been married for two years and then separate, the prenuptial can provide for an amount of money to be paid to the dependent spouse. The prenuptial agreement can also specify that the amount of remuneration should increase for each year of the marriage. This formula usually ends after 10 years. For example, after two years of marriage, the dependent spouse might receive $20,000, but after nine years of marriage the dependent spouse could receive $100,000. The inclusion of these types of provisions in the premarital agreement can avoid the dependent spouse contending that he or she was treated unfairly in the signing of the premarital agreement.

What About a Postnuptial Agreement

Postnuptial agreements are even rarer and are perhaps even a bit odd. From my experience, postnuptial agreements are almost always a result of some major event during the marriage. Generally, this event is something that causes the parties to reassess their positions in the marriage. With this event, some married couples will conclude that there should be a mutual decision that to carry on with a productive marriage some sacrifices must be made by one of the parties regarding the division of assets.

Most commonly, this often occurs when one of the parties has engaged in sexual activity outside of the marriage and wants to make amends with regard to the property division. Regardless of the reasoning, all the points discussed about prenuptial agreements should also be included in a postnuptial agreement. However, it should be noted that some states do have more restrictions regarding postnuptial agreements. For example, in some states, people are not allowed to do a post-marriage waiver of spousal support. This is true of post-separation support, temporary alimony, or even permanent alimony. In general, this is simply not a valid waiver that can be placed in a postnuptial agreement. This varies by state.

Finally, it's to be hoped that most couples contemplating marriage do not feel they need a pre-marital contract or prenuptial agreement. There are certainly some situations where it might make sense. The same observation is made with respect to a post-nuptial agreement. But in case either a prenuptial or postnuptial agreement is warranted, it is important to carefully consider the points made in this chapter.

Chapter 11

FINANCIALLY SURVIVING AFTER THE DIVORCE

Surviving the Aftermath

We spend a lot of time talking with divorcing spouses about their long-term future financial life. This is one of the most stressful aspects of divorce and a topic that has an impact that carries on well after the divorce is over, for years. We need to flesh out some of our major thoughts on this issue, so there are no surprises after the fact.

From our experience in talking to clients about divorce, they almost always state that they want to continue living exactly as they did before the divorce, and it is up to the attorneys, experts, and everyone else to make sure this happens. Let's say right now that it will not happen. No matter how tough an attorney says they are, or how they say they're going to fight for you, there are two constraining components: The Theoretical Laws of Divorce Economics and the Laws of Divorce.

The Theoretical Laws of Divorce Economics

The Theoretical Laws of Divorce Economics are pretty simple. Everybody needs to bring in more money than they are spending.

Hopefully, as a practical matter, people can bring in more money than they spend, because that way they can save for a rainy day or retirement. If a person spends more money than they bring in, they will have to borrow money in the short run, and most probably go under in the long run. There is no getting around this fact of life.

The bottom line of divorce is that a person's financial life will almost always not be as good after the divorce as before, no matter how much they demand from their attorney. The only exception to this rule might be the top echelon of the super-rich. But for most people, while the emotional and physical aspects of the divorcing spouse might get better, economic things will almost always be a bit tougher. And the reason is simple. Two people living together can share a lot of their costs. This is called overhead. It can cost about the same for two people as one person for the mortgage or rent, the homeowner's or rental insurance, the property taxes, and the utility costs. Food can be purchased in bulk for the whole family. Family health and auto insurance is less than the sum of individual insurance costs. Cars can be shared between family members. Even if both spouses move to smaller residences, the combined costs will likely still be greater than sharing the previous single residence.

The Laws of Divorce Economics hit women particularly hard. Several studies have shown that women, on the average, have a reduction of 35% to 45% in their needs-adjusted income after marital separation. For non-custodial men, men not having primary custody of a child or children after the divorce, the falloff is a little less, but still significant—about a 30% drop in needs-adjusted income. Divorce law tries to make things at least roughly fair, through possible alimony, child support, and the division of assets, but it will be tougher for all from a financial perspective. So, plan for a realistic future. We have a couple of simple recommendations.

An Emotional Shift. First, simply understand that the financial world after divorce will be more difficult. That is simply part of the cost of divorce. For many, this requires a true existential change in emotional outlook. It's a fact that needs emotional acceptance. This understanding of the nature of financial life after divorce also needs to happen prior to the actual divorce. The future financial situation will be different from the past. Just accept this fact and plan for it.

Formally Budget. Put your income and expenses down on paper before making a decision after the divorce to rent an expensive apartment, buy a new high-end car, or go on a celebratory vacation to the Greek islands. Figure out the insurance, maintenance, and gas for the car you want to keep from the marriage. What honestly are your food, utility, and clothing costs going to be? A lot of people think formal budgeting is silly, but going into a divorce is when it's needed the most. Think about where your income is going to come from. How much is going to come into your household from your job, or alimony and child support, or from investments? If you are the spouse obligated to pay alimony and/or child support, this will inevitably be a major increase in your expenses. You need to have an accurate understanding of all this. Budgeting during a divorce should be a regular habit.

Talk to a Financial Expert. Talking though your finances is critical. While some people can budget accurately, from our experience many divorcing spouses either don't want to think about this, since it's a difficult topic, or they're basically math challenged. If either of these apply, then talk to somebody. This can be a family member or friend who understands finance and budgeting better than you, and you feel comfortable talking with about such stuff. Or you can hire a financial planner for a more formal look. But that's another expense. In a previous chapter we mentioned using a Certified

Divorce Financial Analyst (CDFA). They are trained to assist in both pre and post-divorce finances. In any case, for at least the first few years after divorce, you need to stick to a well thought out and comprehensive budget.

Understand the sources of income or, flip side, expenses carefully. Under the laws of divorce: in general the courts only influence three sources of income, particularly in the long-term. First, there is a division of assets which might provide some income, such as rental properties or investment accounts. Second, there is child support, and third, there is alimony or spousal support. Of course, you might also get a job, if the other sources of income aren't enough. In some cases, your ex-spouse's social security credit might also help. We'll discuss each of these in turn.

Sources of Income After Divorce: Start Thinking About a Job Early

Of course, many divorcing couples both have jobs. Hopefully, this will continue after the divorce. Quite often, one of the spouses has stayed at home, while the other has been the primary income earner. There is a general expectation by everybody, however, that both spouses do their best to mitigate against the loss of income or increase in expenses after a divorce, at least in the long-term. For the non-income-earning spouse, this probably means trying to find a job sometime after a divorce.

A non-income earning spouse starts immediately with a disadvantage after divorce. Somebody who has been out of the job market for years while raising a family and managing a household has probably lost an edge in the marketplace. This is true even if they had a license or profession prior to the marriage. Often, women who marry early, out of high school, have never been on the job market. Most people, male or female, if they haven't worked for a while don't have a lot of confidence when reentering the job market. Often, a marriage creates a long career time gap on the resume that employers do look at. Many older partners honestly feel it's too late to enter the job market.

This is why planning for a possible divorce scenario needs to start early. If you think that the marriage is not going well, start to think about job training, going back to school, working part-time to get some experience, re-upping your old practitioner license, and generally getting your foot in some door. Do this well prior to a possible divorce. Start networking at your Church, social club, and among friends who might have job connections. Your relationships matter in this way, as in many others. Since marriage dissolutions can be quick in coming, I would suggest getting trained in areas that have a clear career path, but don't require years of preparation. For example, some areas like becoming medical assistants or dental assistants require less time to be trained. Talk to a job counselor and take their advice to heart.

Also make sure you develop your own credit prior to divorcing. Simply get a credit card in your name. Use it occasionally, and make sure you pay it off each month. Open a small bank account in your name, even for just a couple hundred dollars.

Waiting to the last minute simply does not give you enough time to prepare for entering the job market. This is the key: Start thinking about re-entering the labor market early, well prior to the ultimate separation and divorce, perhaps years in advance. While alimony and other forms of spousal support can certainly help, for shorter-term marriages this type of support may not last long.

As a professor in a business school, I can't tell you how many single mothers come back to school after a divorce. Yet they struggle far more than any other type of student. These desperate students try to balance child obligations, manage their family household obligations, and work as a restaurant server at night while studying to get their degree at the same time. It's just incredible stress. I've had several divorced mothers break down crying in my office when they couldn't make a project deadline or haven't had enough study time to pass an exam.

Waiting to the last minute is never a good strategy. There are hundreds of web sites talking about the problems that women have in finding a job after divorce. But they all seem to focus on the emotional and self-confidence side of the problem. That's important, but it won't alone put you in line for a career. Honestly, you need to get experience, formal training, and orientation to make it in the current job market. You also need to stand financially on your own two feet at some point, and it's far better to start early during the marriage when there is a semblance of financial stability, rather than waiting to begin thinking about this after the final divorce.

Also note that many states have a form of short-term "rehabilitative" alimony to assist the at-risk spouse to become self-supporting. This can include payments for training, education and developing skills to succeed in the job market. If a state does not formally have a rehabilitative alimony designation, job retraining costs can often be incorporated into the general temporary spousal support agreement.

Sources of Income After Divorce: Assets

When thinking about the division of assets discussed in the prior chapter, remember that although all assets have some value, and on the spreadsheet you might get credit for them, not all assets can generate income. Rental properties certainly provide income, a business creates income, investments such as CDs and mutual funds can generate income, and pensions do. But also remember that some of these income generating assets may also have debt and other expenses attached that you need to service to get that income, such as mortgage payments, maintenance costs, HOA fees, and insurance for a rental property. Other hard assets, such as cars, boats, jet skis, and gun collections do not easily create income unless you sell them. And that might be more difficult and time consuming than you think. Just remember all this when considering the division of assets.

As we have discussed, pensions earned during the marriage are also considered a marital asset. If you and your spouse decided to split future pension payments using a "Qualified Domestic Relations Order," or QDRO, you can incorporate this future income into your budgetary thinking.

Sources of Income After Divorce: Child Support

We have touched on the issue of child support many times in this book, since divorce with younger children will certainly involve some form of child support. However, in this chapter we go into a little more detail since child support is, in fact, a source of funds that flows to a household for those receiving the child support.

There is no doubt that whoever receives child support emotionally views it as income to the household, and they budget their expenses accordingly. For those individuals paying child support, it represents a real monthly cash outflow, and one that shouldn't be missed. From our experience, child support is also one of the most frustrating of all payments, not because of a lack of desire to help their children, but due to the amount often calculated. It needs to be understood that the amount of child support is not the fault of your attorney or the court.

As mentioned earlier, for most people child support is based on a formula. There is no way around this. The Federal Family Support Act of 1988 mandated that all states select a uniform method to calculate child support, and now all use some type of formal Child Support Calculator. Anyone can access these calculators. Inputs are typically how much income the parties make (and this is normally gross income—more on that later), how many kids there are, how much time parents have with the kids (often based on number of overnights per year), and other items such as pre-existing child support, health insurance, and other specific child related costs such as special schooling, and so on.

There is not much wiggle room here. As a note, about 40 of the states in the U.S. use the "income shares" or "percentage income shares" model of child support. They are similar, with some minor differences. What's interesting is that the income shares model does not try to figure out the real cost of raising a child but is rather based on a broad definition of income.

There are also some other models, such as the Flat Percentage or Varying Percentage model (used by 6 states) and the Melson Formula (used by 3 states). Your attorney will be intimately familiar with which formula applies to you, and how to calculate it. You can also find child support calculators on the web for every state. In most cases, but not all, child support lasts to age 18 or 19, but in some states may be longer if a child is going to college. It might end earlier if your child is granted "emancipation," such as when joining the military or getting married. Parents can generally create their own child support agreement outside of court, but a judge will need to approve any child related agreements, keeping the best interests of the child or children in mind.

The child support formulas typically apply to couples with somewhat normal income. Most states have a rule that if a couple's income is very high, say over $500,000, or even millions of dollars per year, then child support becomes much more complicated. In these high-income cases, generally a judge will make a support decision based on several factors, including "reasonable needs." Each state, however, is different in these high-income situations. This is when an honest and humane settlement discussion is especially important.

From our experience, very few parents object to helping their kids after divorce. All parents recognize the importance of child support, and they almost always express that to their attorney. The point of contention is usually the amount involved, and the ability to supervise how it may be spent.

As a point of reference, child support formulas have all been developed in a rational manner. It's difficult to argue with the underlying logic to share the costs of raising your kids. The point of debate is really what to include in the definition of income. There is no doubt that currently the definition of what to include as income is designed to increase the amount of child support. Studies have also shown that how different states define the formula significantly impacts the calculated child support. One recent study, for example, entered the same income and child information in all 50 state formulas, and came up with wildly different child support payments. The study found that Massachusetts and Nevada were the highest, and almost three times higher than Virgina, West Virginia and New Jersey. The Northeastern region (except New Jersey), and perhaps surprisingly the southern U.S. states of North Carolina, South Carolina, Georgia, Alabama, Mississippi, Arkansas, and Louisiana had the highest average calculated child support.

In some states, income sources that are included in child support calculations are defined in the state's laws and statutes. Here is a list from FindLaw.com of commonly used sources of income for purposes of child support. This list is not exhaustive.

- Salaries and wages. Including tips, commissions, bonuses, profit sharing, deferred compensation, and severance pay
- Income from overtime and second jobs. Income from contractual agreements. And investment and interest income, including dividends
- Pension income
- Trust or estate income
- Annuities
- Capital gains unless the gain is nonrecurring in some states, in which case it may be necessary to prove at a later time that it occurred only once

- Social Security benefits
- Veterans' benefits
- Military personnel fringe benefits
- National Guard and Reserve drill pay
- Benefits received in place of earned income. Examples: workers' compensation benefits, unemployment insurance benefits, strike pay, and disability insurance benefits
- Gifts and prizes, including lottery and gambling winnings
- Education grants: including fellowships. Or subsidies that are available for personal living expenses and educational expenses
- Alimony/spousal support received
- Income from self-employment

This is about everything that can bring funds into the household. Quite frankly, some of these components don't make a lot of sense. For example, the total income from self-employment (versus a fair market salary from the family business) has already been included in the valuation of the business for the purpose of divisible assets. Likewise, many of the components, such as family gifts, educational grants, and lottery winnings are specific to a particular year (and luck) and certainly not recurring.

It also makes no sense to me to include capital gains for several reasons. Capital gains is an accounting measure between what one sells an asset for and the depreciated cost of that asset. Capital gains are not recurring but are typically a very infrequent event upon the sale of an asset. The asset that's being sold has already been incorporated into the division of assets for the divorce. Ultimately selling an asset also decreases the asset base of the spouse. Considered opinions can differ on such matters, but what always matters is following the law in your own state.

This broad definition of income for child support often creates a huge problem of constantly trying to change child support amounts each year. This involves going back to court. Unfortunately, it also encourages the spouse with the highest income to hide some of their income, not because they don't want to help their kids but because the definition of income is simply far too broad. This is particularly true when there is a small family business involved. In these cases, there is almost always a debate as to how much money (combination of salary, bonus, profit, and personal expenses being paid by the business) is actually being earned by the in-spouse from the business. In these cases, hiding income is a real problem when calculating child support.

Regardless of how we think about this, the law is the law, and the formula is the formula. Child support, while inevitably creating household income for one party, will certainly also result in a large expense for the other party. Just make sure this issue is incorporated into the budgeting process, regardless of which side of the child support fence you may be on.

Also, remember, the discussion of child support issues in this chapter only refers to the financial aspect of long-term survival after divorce. Of course, issues of child support also involve visitation, custody, enforcement, and a whole bunch of other matters discussed earlier. Child support can be negotiated by the parties in a settlement but will normally need to be approved by the judge who will evaluate the child support agreement as to the "best interest of the children."

Sources of Income After Divorce: Alimony or Long-Term Spousal Support

In addition to short term spousal support and rehabilitative alimony, all states have some form of longer "durational" spousal maintenance. Different states tend to call these durational payments different things, such as alimony, long-term spousal support, spousal maintenance, or alimony *in futuro* (for the future).

How is Alimony Calculated? In general, alimony is going to be based on a combination of things including the length of the marriage, the ability of one spouse to pay alimony, the standard of living enjoyed by the receiving spouse when married, the spouses' ages, their contributions to raising children, each spouse's future earning capacity, the education levels of the spouses, health insurance costs, and whether a spouse contributed to maintaining the household or putting the other spouse through college.

Note that some states, such a Virginia, have a list of factors that need to be considered as part of state law. Other states allow more discretion. However, for states that have more discretion, there are often still guidelines. For example, the American Association of Matrimonial Lawyers has suggested a guideline that it takes 30% of gross annual income of the person paying alimony minus 20% of the gross annual income of the recipient to estimate an appropriate alimony.

Often, if one spouse committed adultery that led to the marital breakup, that can also be considered in determining, or even negating, the right for long-term spousal support depending on who was the offending party. But adulterous acts that happen long before separation and seemed to have been dealt with during the marriage, have less weight. Actions such as knowingly causing physical harm to a child or the other spouse will also be considered.

Many states treat alimony, spousal support, or spousal maintenance as you would child support. There are strict guidelines, and support is determined by a formula based on income and length of marriage. In these states, like in the case of child support, there are also durational support or alimony calculators. In these states, you are thus paid alimony for a certain amount of time according to a formula.

Other states give much more discretion to the court. Frankly we prefer a case-by-case determination. After all, we're all different and so are our circumstances. In non-formula states, however, there are still often general "rules of thumb." But even these rules of thumb can vary from state to state, and from county to county. Some states, such as Texas, also place limits on how much alimony can be ordered.

What is the Length of Alimony? One often hears the rule of thumb that alimony or long-term spousal support should be one-half the length of the marriage, but every state is different.

For example, in North Carolina we often see that a marriage of less duration than 10 years results in spousal support payments for half the length of the marriage. If the marriage is 10 to 20-years long, then spousal support is about 75 percent of the marriage. For marriages longer than 20 years, spousal support tends to be almost permanent. Many states have similar guidelines, although the percentages might be a little different. In Florida, for example, one often reads that for marriages between 10 and 20 years, alimony is typically 60%, while for marriages longer than 20 years the length is generally 75%. Some states have more formal requirements for the minimum length of a marriage to receive alimony, such as 3 years or more. In Indiana, alimony cannot generally be permanent, but rather often needs to have an ending date. In Texas, marriages longer than 30 years receive support generally for no more than 10 years. So, understand, there is a lot of variation in the duration and amount of alimony depending on the state. This is something that needs to be understood clearly and discussed with your attorney. This is particularly important since spousal support is generally a large part of the post-divorce financial picture for both parties, the recipient and the payor.

However, it's also crucial to realize that as in most things in the law, nothing is permanent. In most states, support ends at the court ordered date, or with the death of either party, or at the remarriage of the recipient spouse. Most states also end alimony if the recipient person romantically co-habituates with a partner, but this co-habitation needs to be proven to the court and often needs to be filed within a certain date after being discovered.

In long-term marriages of over 20 years, the couples are, of course, older, and the support is often limited by age. When you hit your 70's or 80's, hopefully people have planned not to depend completely on the ex-spouse's income, and there are other sufficient income generating assets and pensions that will be divided through the property settlement.

Almost always, if there are significant changes in circumstances, such as an involuntary job loss, or a new long-term disability or disease resulting in significant medical expenses, the courts will consider a change in long-term alimony.

Enforcement of alimony payments is somewhat like child support, although there are some differences between states. In general, in many states, judges can order wage garnishment, property confiscation, fines, and even jail time for lack of payment, under certain situations.

Can Alimony be Negotiation Between the Parties? As with everything we have discussed in this book, spousal support does not have to be decided by the courts. The individual parties can agree to a spousal support arrangement, which then only needs to be accepted by the court. However, this becomes a contract and is often referred to as "contractual alimony." This is probably the most humane and agreeable manner to manage the spousal support issue. But it requires flexibility and understanding by all parties involved. While we strongly support working out spousal support agreements, there are generally some basic clauses that need to be included in negotiated spousal support agreements. These include a modification clause, so changes can be made in the future if there is a significant change in circumstances. If the state has spousal support guidelines, then the parties should acknowledge they were aware of the guidelines and nobody involved in the agreement was being coerced. Your attorney will need to be involved in the writing up of any negotiated spousal support agreements. Also, courts can generally reject the spousal support agreements if they consider them to be unfair

Sources of Income After Divorce: Social Security and Government Assistance

Government Assistance Programs. For individuals and families that are financially struggling after divorce, there are various government assistance programs, such as Welfare, Temporary Assistance for Needy Families (TANF), food assistance (SNAP), emergency housing, assistance with utility expenses, school lunch programs, Medicaid, and other assistance programs if you or a dependent child might be disabled. Some of these programs are federal in nature, while many of them are run at the state level and may have different procedures and benefits across states. These programs are designed to assist individuals and families in need.

The range and requirements for the different government assistance programs are beyond this short book, but there are many local social service advisors and offices that can help. There are also many websites, such as usa.gov/benefits that can point you in the right direction. If you qualify for these assistance programs, you should apply. Most of the applications for government assistance are now online, although you can also make appointments at the local social services offices.

The key thing when it comes to divorce is to remember that it often takes several months after you apply before these assistance programs are approved, or they might ask for additional documentation during the application process. So, if you are getting divorced or separated, and you qualify for some of these programs, start the process immediately—maybe even before separating. Check the various webpages, make some phone calls, or talk to a social services officer to find out what the requirements are, how to apply, and what documentation you need.

Social Security Benefits. The final topic is Social Security benefits. This is a topic that surprisingly few divorcing couples know much about. In some cases, a divorced spouse has a right to obtain social security benefits earned by the other spouse's work credit. This right, however, does not reduce the earning spouse's social security benefits, so there is no loss to the other spouse. In fact, your ex doesn't have to even know you have applied and are receiving social security benefits based upon their work history.

There are a lot of rules, however, for this to happen. *Forbes* has had a very good summary of the basic rules, which are quoted here word for word. (For the original source, go to: https://www.forbes.com/sites/heatherlocus/2021/10/21/ a-comprehensive-guide-to-social-security-after-divorce/). These are the rules:

1. There are no decisions to make or filing requirements during the divorce. The benefits are determined by the Social Security Administration when you get to age 62+ so this is a rare financial issue you can put off thinking about until well after the divorce is finalized if you are younger than 62.
2. No court order is necessary—all you need is proof you were married for at least 10 years and proof you are now divorced.
3. Your former spouse's benefits are not affected at all by your claim—they don't even have to know you are filing on their work history!
4. Benefits can be received while your ex-spouse is alive as well as after they die.
5. At full retirement age, benefits are a percentage (typically 50%) of your ex-spouse's social security benefits.

How do I qualify as an ex-spouse? To be eligible, given your ex-spouse's work history, all the following must apply:

- Your marriage lasted 10 years or longer.
- You are not currently married (unless you were over age 60 when the remarriage occurred).
- You are 62 years or older (unless you're disabled, or your ex-spouse is deceased).
- Your ex-spouse's benefit is greater than any you would receive based on your own working record (you can't double dip).
- Your ex-spouse is entitled to Social Security retirement or disability benefits.

The five key issues on receiving social security benefits are (1) a 10 year marriage or longer, (2) You can't be remarried (unless over 60), (3) your ex-spouse's benefit is greater than you own benefits based on your work experience, (4) you can't collect until age 62, and (5) an ex-spouse receiving benefits does not reduce the other spouse's right to their own social security benefits. Remember, social security doesn't allow "double-dipping." You get the highest benefit, but not a combination of yours and your ex's benefit.

Given these rules, for certain marriages there is a strategic way to manage this process for the benefit of all. For example, suppose the divorcing partners are older, one partner has been the wage earner, and the length of the marriage is close to 10 years. Then perhaps both parties could agree to hold off divorcing until the 10-year marriage requirement is met. It makes sense. But make sure you check the current regulations, since given the future difficulties in funding social security, the government is always tweaking the rules. Even the basic rules discussed above have various exceptions, such as being disabled. There are also some oddities if your ex dies, or you remarry and then divorce again. Just be aware of these possible benefits if contemplating divorce, particularly for older couples.

Final Thoughts on Long-Term Financial Survival After Divorce

As we have pointed out, it's almost aways true that the long-term financial situation after separation and divorce will not be the same as during the marriage. Some of the emotional aspects of your life might certainly be better, but financially—probably not. The theoretical laws of divorce economics will ultimately come into play. Almost certainly, there will be a decrease in your needs-adjusted income, for both former partners—for the higher income spouse who might have to cover alimony and child support, as well as for lower-income generating spouse, since both simply can't live separated in the same economic manner they did while married. This is just the way it is for nearly every case.

But this does not need to be devastating if a few basic strategies are followed. First, plan early, particularly if you will need to find a job after the divorce. Start thinking about training programs, building your credit, and targeting a career path before separating. Once separated, the stress of managing your own household can often become too great to move forward easily into a desired career.

If you are the primary income-earning spouse in a dissolving marriage, it can be wise to work with the other spouse to help get them going in the right direction financially. That is the humane way to engage in this aspect of the process.

Second, remember to budget, budget, and budget. Put your anticipated income and expenses down on paper. It's worth the trouble. The income side tends to be fairly fixed in these situations, but you can manage and control some of your expenses with careful planning. And don't be afraid of asking for some help from professionals or friends and family to assist you in understanding budgets and how they best can be used.

Third, realize that, depending on the length of marriage, and whether children are involved, some sources of long-term income such as alimony and child support will ultimately end. You need to take that into account. If you are the receiving spouse and your alimony ends in 5 years, think twice about committing yourself to a 30-year mortgage that exceeds your other income sources. Just be smart. Think ahead.

And fourth, be creative in your thinking. Can you spend some time back at your parents' house while getting back on your feet or going through a job training program at the local community college, or getting your prior professional certification current? Do you qualify for some type of government assistance programs? Can you call on a network of friends or family to help you find a job? Are there other coping strategies that you can use in the short-term?

Obviously, remarriage (or "re-partnering") is often considered a coping strategy, but research has found that rebound partnerships, particularly when done mostly for financial reasons, tend to be very short-lived and unhappy. Just be smart, not desperate, in your thinking. Life contains more possibilities than we tend to see at any given time. And above all, plan what's best for you in the long-run, and if children are involved, what's best for the overall family situation.

Chapter 12

Final Thoughts

Two Perspectives

This book was written by two authors from very different backgrounds, careers, and educational degrees. One of us has a law degree and has worked in family law for over 40 years. The other has a doctorate in business and economics, and has worked around financial, small business, management, and valuation issues for 40 years. One of us grew up in North Carolina, while the other grew up in San Diego, California. One of us is a lifelong Democrat, and the other a lifelong Republican. One of us is Catholic and the other is Protestant.

Despite these differences, the two authors of this book have three very important common traits. First, we both have a lot of experience working with thousands of clients going through a marital dissolution. Combined, we have over eighty years of experience dealing with the issues discussed in this book. This type of experience does create an opportunity for getting a real sense of the different behaviors and outcomes that are possible. Second, both of us are dedicated, and committed, and have personalities that want to see problems solved, no matter how frustrating. Marital problems lead to divorce, and divorce creates a whole new set of problems. Problems, however, can be dealt with.

Thirdly, we both like to solve problems in the most effective manner possible. Perhaps this is because both of us played varsity sports in high school and college and continued to play competitive sports until injury or other health issues slowed us down in the last couple of years. Perhaps it's just in the DNA. Finally, and most importantly, both of us believe that divorce, in spite of its inherently ugly and unfortunate nature, can be managed in a wise, civilized, and even humane manner by both parties. It's actually the best option open to everyone going through such a difficult process.

For this reason, each of us will give some final, quick comments from our different perspectives.

Final Comments from the Divorce Attorney, Jim

I can only hope that this book will help people understand the process of divorce and guide them through the winding path in a way that will not only salvage their self-respect, but also their family connections, and perhaps even a relationship with their ex-spouse. If you have children, you are inexplicably and inextricably bound to each other for the rest of your lives. While you will ultimately go your own way, your children, and even your history of being together as a married couple will be with you for the rest of your life. That ex-spouse will always be a part of your memories and will, believe it or not, have a great impact on how you choose your future relationships. Some of you may be divorced and married on several occasions during your life, some once, and some never. If you act wisely, humanely, fairly, sanely, spiritually, and always seek to do the right thing, you will likely enjoy a mostly happy and controversy free life.

There's a reason that domestic lawyers are hated, sometimes

shot or killed, emotionally burned out from their profession, and have nervous breakdowns, or become alcoholics or drug addicts. It's a profession that wears people out. If we treat each other with respect, we can survive together through this challenging and often traumatic process.

In many ways, this book is meant for lawyers as much as it is for clients, so that we can better understand each other and practice better law and in a way in which our children will not look back as adults and not have us as their example of who they do not want to be.

Final Comments from the Financial and Businessperson, Craig

I personally believe that marriage has a spiritual component, above and beyond the civil contract. We have purposely not brought faith, religion, and the spiritual perspective into this book. Rather we have concentrated on the underlying concept of humaneness and civilized behavior. All of us, with faith or without it, can act in a humane way. It's often easy to act in such a manner when things are going your way, but true humaneness really shows when things get tough. Divorce is tough.

At the front end of this book, we talked about where the word "humane" comes from. It means action which is proper to being human. In means action which is defined as civilized behavior. I firmly believe that divorce, when it's necessary, needs to be done in a humane and civilized manner. This is particularly true when there are children involved. But even if children are not part of the equation, there are proper behaviors, for this and any situation. Everybody will be better off for this in the end.

People often forget that the definition of "humaneness" also involves a component of knowledge. One cannot be fully humane without knowledge. That is a major reason I personally got involved with this book—to help make sure that readers can better understand the complex process of a marital dissolution, from the complicated legal perspectives to the many financial angles. My specialty is financial, business, and economic issues. I'm not an attorney, but these financial issues are very complex matters for most people going through the pain of divorce. Being taken advantage of in a divorce situation, whether by your "ex", the attorneys involved, or other advisors you might consult, will be minimized or prevented by having the right knowledge and understanding of the process and possibilities it offers for the good of all parties involved.

Whether the reader is somebody unfortunately going through a divorce, just thinking about it, or simply advising a friend or family member, please keep in mind and consider carefully the issues we have raised.

Legal

Disclaimer

Although the publisher and the author have made every effort to ensure that the information in this book was correct at press time and while this publication is designed to provide accurate information in regard to the subject matter covered, the publisher and the author assume no responsibility for errors, inaccuracies, omissions, or any other inconsistencies herein and hereby disclaim any liability to any party for any loss, damage, or disruption caused by errors or omissions, whether such errors or omissions result from negligence, accident, or any other cause.

This publication is meant as a source of valuable information for the reader, however it is not meant as a substitute for direct expert assistance. If such level of assistance is required, the services of a competent professional should be sought.

About The Authors

Jim Lea:

As the legal expert of this team, Jim Lea is in his 44th year of practicing law. The last 30 years have been dominated by his family law practice along with extensive civil litigation. Jim holds an "A" rating by Martindale Hubbell, the leading lawyers rating service. In the past 20 years Jim has been recognized in the area of Family Law as one of the best in his field in publications such as *US News and World Report* "Best Lawyers in America" and "Best Law Firms in America" as well as "Super Lawyers" and *North Carolina Business Magazine's* "Legal Elite."

Craig Galbraith:

The other author, Dr. Craig Galbraith, holds the Duke Progress Energy/Betty Cameron Distinguished Professorship at the University of North Carolina Wilmington, He is also the senior partner in *Galbraith Forensic & Economic Sciences*, LLC. He has been a court-qualified expert and consultant in hundreds of divorce cases involving businesses, pensions, investments, and many other financial issues that surface during divorce proceedings. He received his Ph.D. in management and economics from Purdue University and also holds graduate degrees in both molecular biology and operations management.

Book the Authors of
The Humane Divorce: Breaking Up Without Breaking Down
for Your Next Event

Divorce is often treated as a legal transaction – but it is fundamentally a human experience. *The Humane Divorce* explores the psychological, emotional, financial, and relational dimensions of divorce in ways that empower individuals, families, and professionals to navigate this transition with empathy, intelligence, and dignity.

James Lea and Craig Galbraith dismantle outdated notions of conflict-driven separations and invite audiences to reimagine divorce as a process rooted in self-awareness, ethical decision-making, and future-focused collaboration.

Live Panels, Fireside Chats, Book Readings, or Virtual Dialogues

Customize your event: from intimate panels to large-scale conferences, the team will collaborate to create a compelling, interactive experience.

Featured Topics:
- The Humane Divorce: Rethinking the End of a Marriage
- Divorcing with Children: Building Stability in Uncertain Times
- Love, Law, and Letting Go

Bring *The Humane Divorce* to your stage, boardroom, classroom, or community and help your audience discover how to navigate one of life's biggest challenges with courage, civility, and compassion.

Inquire about Booking:
marketing@thehumanedivorce.com
Learn more at www.thehumanedivorce.com

Book Sales can be incorporated into speaking events.

The Humane Divorce: Breaking Up Without Breaking Down available on Amazon and wherever books are sold.